The Holy Spirit
in
Today's World

The Holy Spirit
in
Today's World

DAVID ALLAN HUBBARD

WORD BOOKS, Publisher
Waco, Texas

Contents

Introduction

This book approaches the work of the Holy Spirit from a biblical perspective, designedly so. The Holy Spirit has not lacked attention among contemporary Christians. The past two decades have seen a resurgence of interest in the Spirit of God and, with that interest, a spate of literature.

But more often than not, the perspective from which the books, pamphlets, and magazines have been written is experiential. Testimony after testimony has been shared; experience after experience has been recounted; biography after biography has been analyzed. And with considerable profit to the Church in strengthened faith and renewed hope in God's power and purposes.

More is needed, however. Since it is God we talk about when we discuss the Spirit's activity, where can we go but to the Bible to gain our basic understanding? We can no more base our doctrine of the Holy Spirit on our experience alone than we can develop a doctrine of creation on the basis of an ocean sunset or an autumn drive through the mountains. Such experiences are important. They confirm and illustrate what we have learned. But when it comes to God, we do our learning from the Bible where he has spoken fully and clearly of himself.

This is a touchy subject—what the Bible teaches about the Holy Spirit. I was reminded of this as soon as I announced this topic for a series of radio messages on our international broadcast, "The Joyful Sound." When these chapters were first heard as radio talks, managers of radio stations began to write or phone. How was I going to handle the topic? Was I going to take stands on some of the controversial issues? These and other questions were on their minds. Through the years I have spoken on many topics with scarcely a shrug

7

from the station managers. But when the topic was the Holy Spirit, the situation was different.

To the concerns of people who have strong feelings about the issues involved, I have tried to be sensitive. My aim has been to say neither less nor more than what the New Testament teaches about the acts of God the Holy Spirit.

Still I have done this with an obvious *sense of incompleteness*. When the subject is God, how can one feel otherwise? There are aspects of his person and work that I have not touched upon or only pointed to. But what I consider the main facets and the key passages in which they are reflected I have tried to look at, with the limitations imposed by the radio format.

The brevity and chattiness of these chapters will not, I hope, obscure the *sense of importance* which I feel about the topic. In our churches and study groups today, the subject of the Holy Spirit is too frequently dealt with in isolation from other doctrines. The relationship of the Spirit to the Father and the Son is sometimes ignored. The specific role which the Spirit plays in God's redemptive program must be considered. So must the close ties between the Spirit and the Scriptures and between the Spirit and the Church.

The Bible calls us to walk a narrow line between fear of fanaticism on the one hand and presumptuousness on the other. There are well-meaning but timid souls within the Church who shy away from a study of the Spirit's gifts and power because they are aware of the excesses of emotionalism to which some believers are prone. There are other equally well-meaning brothers and sisters who boast some special claim on the Spirit that enables them to advertise miracles nightly at 7:30 or to predict the turn of future events in world history as well as the lives of their followers.

Biblical teaching, as I see it, lies between these extremes. The Holy Spirit is not in our employ; we are in his. He is Lord of the Church. We must let him work on his terms and schedule. We cannot manipulate his power or program his activities. But because he is Lord, we must be open to whatever he wants to do, receptive to whatever gifts he sends, responsive to whatever priorities he sets.

My wife, Ruth, good friend and loyal critic, has worked over these chapters, making sure the transition from oral to written form is smooth and typing the manuscript. Together we send it out with the hope that God's Spirit, about whose mysteries it dares to speak, will be pleased to use it for the good of his people.

Matthew 28:16–20
2 Corinthians 13:14
John 14:15–31

1. The Spirit Is a Person

Now the eleven disciples went to Galilee, to the mountain to which Jesus had directed them. And when they saw him they worshiped him; but some doubted. And Jesus came and said to them, "All authority in heaven and on earth has been given to me. Go therefore and make disciples of all nations, baptizing them in the name of the Father and of the Son and of the Holy Spirit, teaching them to observe all that I have commanded you; and lo, I am with you always, to the close of the age" (Matt. 28:16–20).

The grace of the Lord Jesus Christ and the love of God and the fellowship of the Holy Spirit be with you all (2 Cor. 13:14).

The man raised his hand in the discussion group. It was time for questions and comments. My informal talk had dealt with the Holy Spirit and what the Bible says about him. I called on the man, and then stood in blank surprise as he made his point: "The names bother me," he blurted out. "*Ghost* and *Spirit* are such vague terms—and a little spooky. Why can't we call the Holy Spirit the *influence* of God?"

I suppose I had a puzzled look on my face as I mulled over his question in my mind. What made me hesitate as I answered was the novelty of the question. No one had ever asked me that before. I had never thought about the difficulties people in today's world may have with the term Spirit. The word Ghost is Old English, and we don't use that much any more except in our hymns. Ghost reminds us of haunted houses and Halloween. But Spirit, Holy Spirit—I had never met anyone who was bothered by that term.

To the man who had raised the question I tried to make just one point. "What is crucial," I answered, "is for us to

11

remember that the Holy Spirit is a person." The danger with using a term like *influence* or *power* or *force* of the Spirit is that we will lose track of his personality. We will reduce him in our thinking to a thing, an it, a tool.

If it is harmful to our relationships with people to treat them as things, if it mars their dignity and hampers their humanity for us to treat persons as tools or toys, think how dangerous it must be for us to view God the Holy Spirit as just an influence. It is true that God works even where his nature and work are not understood. But this does not mean that we should not try hard to understand who he is and what he does.

One great difficulty we have is picturing personality without a face and body to tie it to. When you think of a close relative or a firm friend you picture a face and a form. Tall and thin you see him, with bushy hair, bright eyes, and a crooked, boyish smile. His personality and his looks are tied up in a bundle. You don't think of a collection of abstract traits when you reflect on those dear to you. Kindness, generosity, courage, wisdom, understanding, gentleness are hard to picture apart from persons in whom these traits dwell and through whom they are expressed.

With the Holy Spirit we have a problem. How do we picture him? The Bible uses symbols to describe the Spirit's work—symbols like a dove, a mighty wind, tongues of fire, new wine, oil used in anointing. But these only tell what the Holy Spirit is *like*, not what he *is*. They are word pictures of his work, poetic descriptions of the peace, power, and joy that he brings.

We have a problem to be sure. We want to talk about God's Spirit as a person, yet we cannot see him. No photographer can capture his portrait on film; no artist can sketch his silhouette on canvas.

Yet he is a person. The problem of understanding this is *our* problem, a product of our human limitations, evidence of our dim perceptiveness. If we look at what is involved in personality closely enough, we will realize that face and form—bodily existence—are not as central as it may seem. Perhaps the telephone is an illustration of this. Every day, especially in business, men and women carry on lengthy, personal, even intimate conversations with other men and women whom they have never met, whom they would not recognize if they bumped into each other on the street. They know each other well, these telephone friends. Each could give a fairly accurate sketch of the other's personality—his likes and dislikes, his basic feelings and attitudes, his strong points and weaknesses. With only the sound of a voice and the power of the spoken word, a whole profile of personality is being communicated.

So it is with God's Spirit. We neither see him nor touch him; yet by hearing his words in the Scriptures and noting what Jesus and his apostles have said about him, we can begin to understand and appreciate his personality. The Holy Spirit is a person—that's the point we want to see. The Scriptures make this clear in a number of ways: first, by stressing the deity of the Holy Spirit; second, by connecting the mission of the Holy Spirit to the mission of Jesus; third, by describing the Holy Spirit's ministry in the Church.

The Holy Spirit Is God

Some of Jesus' final words to his disciples help to bring our first point into sharp focus: "And Jesus came and said to them, 'All authority in heaven and on earth has been given to me. Go therefore and make disciples of all nations, baptizing them in the name of the Father and of the Son and of the Holy Spirit, teaching them to observe all that I have commanded you; and lo, I am with you always, to the close of the age' " (Matt. 28:18–20).

"Baptizing them in the name of the Father and of the Son and of the Holy Spirit"—that's the clause we want to catch. New disciples, turning to God from idols, sloughing off their pagan past, gratefully declaring their new allegiance by their baptism—they confess their faith in one God. Jesus, of all people, was not a polytheist! He did not teach that there were *many* gods. Yet he had introduced the human family to a richer, deeper knowledge of God, God who is Father, Son, Holy Spirit—one God yet three persons.

That the Father is divine needs no arguing. "Our Father who art in heaven, hallowed be thy name" Jesus taught his disciples to pray. The Father in heaven with the holy name to whom we pray, what else could he be but deity?

And Jesus bore witness to his own deity. The great commission itself is sufficient proof of this. "All authority" is what Jesus claims, as he commands the Church of God to go about its world-wide work. And he promises to go with them everywhere, to the close of the age. Presumptuous, even brash, this authority, this command, this promise, unless Jesus is divine.

Linked to the mention of the Father, who is surely divine, and the Son, whose deity shines through the passage, is the Holy Spirit. Unless the Holy Spirit is God also, the words of Jesus are worse than nonsense; they are blasphemy. Idolatry it would be to join the name of anything or anyone except deity to the names of the Father and the Son. Baptism in the *name* of God implies a commitment of allegiance to and worship of God. The obvious intent of Jesus' command is that Christians are to honor and adore the Father, the Son, the Holy Spirit as God. One God, three persons. The Holy Spirit is a person, because he is God.

If the God of the Bible is not a person, no one is. If the God who chose Abraham and his family to serve him who guided their steps and answered their prayers and gave them his Word is not a person, then the whole idea of personhood is foolishness. If the God who showed his holiness, power, and love in his Son, Jesus, is not a person, then ours is a world of *things* in which no persons exist. To love, to choose, to feel, to think, to understand, to plan, to care, to remember— these are the traits of personhood. No one does them better than God. The Holy Spirit is a person, because he is God.

The Holy Spirit Carries on the Work of Jesus

Not an instrument, a force, an attitude, an atmosphere, an influence, the Holy Spirit is a person. We see his personhood in the way he carries out Jesus' mission. Again, some of Jesus' last words are important to us here: "If you love me, you will keep my commandments. And I will pray the Father, and he will give you another Counselor, to be with you for ever, even the Spirit of truth, whom the world cannot receive, because it neither sees him nor knows him; you know him, for he dwells with you, and will be in you" (John 14:15–17).

Another Counselor Jesus promised, another like himself. "He will teach you all things, and bring to your remembrance all that I have said to you" (John 14:26). Counseling, teaching, reminding—these are the tasks of a person, a person like Jesus, without the limitations his flesh put upon him. When Jesus was in Caesarea Philippi with his disciples, he could not at the same time be in Bethany with Mary, Martha, and Lazarus. Part of the limitation he took upon himself when he became man was that he could only be in one place at one time. The Holy Spirit, every bit as much a person as Jesus, does not have this limitation. As the church grew in numbers and spread in location, the Spirit was there, carrying on Jesus' work, with no loss in personal touch or in effectiveness.

The Holy Spirit is a person. As God, he has to be. And he could not have carried out the mission of Jesus Christ unless he were.

The Holy Spirit Ministers to the Church

In his beautiful benediction to the Corinthian church, Paul makes a point that should be added here: "The grace of the Lord Jesus Christ and the love of God and the fellowship of the Holy Spirit be with you all" (2 Cor. 13:14). Personal terms all of these are. Who can show grace by granting forgiveness except a person like the Lord Jesus Christ, God's Son? Who can demonstrate his love except a person like God the Father, who sent his Son to accomplish our salvation? And who can promote fellowship among God's people except a person like God the Holy Spirit, who knits the Church together in the common experience of faith and forgiveness?

The fellowship that the Spirit produces is the enjoyment of what we have in common as Christians. It is not a fellowship based on a congenial culture, a uniform political outlook, an agreement about economic theories. It is not a fellowship of taste and opinion about fashions or fads. It is a fellowship in faith, in worship, in obedience, in mission. It is a fellowship that only the Godhead can initiate and sustain. It is the fellowship of the Holy Spirit, the personal Holy Spirit, the Holy Spirit who is a person, working in and among the persons who have trusted in God through the Lord Jesus Christ.

Three things need to be said in conclusion. First, because the Holy Spirit is God, everything the Bible says about God's character applies to him. God's special kind of love, God's unique brand of holiness, God's abundant power, God's amazing goodness, God's steady faithfulness—all these and more are what the Holy Spirit is and has. Think of it: God the Holy Spirit, who carries on the program designed and implemented by the Father and the Son, has their same concern and ability.

Second, because the Holy Spirit carries out the mission of Christ, we can count on Christ's presence in our midst to meet every basic need of ours. The Spirit reminds us of Christ's love, administers to us Christ's forgiveness, fills us with Christ's power, rebukes us with Christ's wisdom, instructs us in Christ's truth, heals us with Christ's comfort. Bank on it: Christ's own emissary, full of the same power and compassion, is in our midst. He speaks to us through the Scriptures; he bends our wills to yield to the will of God.

Third, because the Holy Spirit ministers in his Church, we can have true fellowship with God and each other. The Spirit lifts us above our prejudices, puts down our likes and dislikes, glues us together in Christian love and concern. Rejoice in it: God the Holy Spirit is breaking down barriers and teaching us that we are one through him. Because he is God, he is more personal even than we are. As God in person, he is working night and day to make us the persons God wants us to be.

Prayer: Heavenly Father, we are idolaters unless God the Holy Spirit teaches us to worship you; we are stupidly confused unless the Spirit of truth opens our eyes to understand your gospel and its demands of discipleship; we are hopelessly divided unless your Spirit knits us together in full fellowship. Free us to let him work, through Jesus Christ our Lord. Amen.

Matthew 3:11–17
John 1:29–34
1 Corinthians 12:12–13

2. The Spirit Baptizes the Church

"I baptize you with water for repentance, but he who is coming after me is mightier than I, whose sandals I am not worthy to carry; he will baptize you with the Holy Spirit and with fire. His winnowing fork is in his hand, and he will clear his threshing floor and gather his wheat into the granary, but the chaff he will burn with unquenchable fire."

Then Jesus came from Galilee to the Jordan to John, to be baptized by him. John would have prevented him, saying, "I need to be baptized by you, and do you come to me?" But Jesus answered him, "Let it be so now; for thus it is fitting for us to fulfil all righteousness." Then he consented. And when Jesus was baptized, he went up immediately from the water, and behold, the heavens opened and he saw the Spirit of God descending like a dove, and alighting on him; and lo, a voice from heaven, saying, "This is my beloved Son, with whom I am well pleased" (Matt. 3:11–17).

For just as the body is one and has many members, and all the members of the body, though many, are one body, so it is with Christ. For by one Spirit we were all baptized into one body—Jews or Greeks, slaves or free—and all were made to drink of one Spirit (1 Cor. 12:12–13).

Those were great days by the banks of the Jordan. From the towns of southern Judea like Hebron and Bethlehem, men and women were coming. And from Galilee to the north, they came—from Bethsaida and Capernaum, from Neapolis and Samaria. And above all from Jerusalem they walked down, by the scores and by the hundreds.

The banks of the river east of Jericho were crowded with bystanders. The center of attraction was a stern man with shaggy beard and fiery eyes. His garb was austere—a cloak woven of camel's hair, cinched at the waist with a leather belt. And his diet was fit for a desert nomad—locusts and wild honey.

It was not to gawk at his garment or to savor his diet that the crowds came. It was to hear his preaching. Not since Jeremiah bearded the kings and priests of Judah six hundred years before, had any prophet made such an impact on the public.

John the Baptist, men called him, the son of Zechariah, the priest, and his wife, Elizabeth. Like a meteor he had come upon the scene, full of power and conviction, a power and conviction that could be credited to the Holy Spirit alone. Like Moses and Elijah before him, he had been toughened for his tasks by the rigors of the desert. In the austerity and isolation of the trackless wastes he had brooded on his mission and mulled over the meaning of his call.

Now the isolation was over, the years of preparation past. The Messiah was standing in the wings and his chief herald had work to do as

"The voice of one crying in the wilderness:
Prepare the way of the Lord,
make his paths straight" (Matt. 3:3).

John's message was as stern as his manner: "Repent, for the kingdom of heaven is at hand" (Matt. 3:2).

Just what brought the crowds is hard to say. Curiosity was undoubtedly part of it—the lure of this unusual character, with his awesome demeanor. Part of it may have been political ambition, the hope that John's kingdom would mean political freedom from Roman domination.

But beyond these reasons, some of the crowds came out of spiritual hunger. Fed up with the legalism of the Pharisees, unimpressed by the opportunism of the Sadducees, disenchanted by the sense of God's remoteness—they came; they heard; they believed. Into the waters of the Jordan they went. Repenting of their sins, renouncing their old ways, they were baptized. Many of them became followers of John.

This was just what John did not want. His baptism had its place, but something better was coming: "I baptize you with water for repentance, but he who is coming after me is mightier than I, whose sandals I am not worthy to carry; he will baptize you with the Holy Spirit and with fire" (Matt. 3:11).

The Great Transition

Nowhere did the greatness of John the Baptist shine more brightly than in his humility. In the presence of God's Messiah, John knew his place; he understood his mission. The baptism with water for repentance was important. It reminded John's countrymen of their need for cleansing; it spurred them to change their selfish, sinful ways; it drew them up short and made them face God's kingly claim upon their lives.

But something more was needed. Man's sins lay deeper than John's baptism could reach; the stains of rebellion were not soluble in water. Repentance and cleansing were good; faith and eternal life were better. John's announcement marked a great transition. From that time forward the spotlight was to be on Jesus, God's Son and Messiah, not on John, who was God's messenger and herald.

Not that Jesus rejected water baptism. To the contrary, Jesus insisted that John baptize him despite John's protests. "I need to be baptized by you," John acknowledged, "and do you come to me?" Jesus' answer was direct: "Let it be so now; for thus it is fitting for us to fulfill all righteousness" (Matt. 3:14–15). In his compassion for us, Jesus entered into all our needs, including our need to demonstrate our full dependence upon God in baptism.

The transition from John's ministry to Jesus' ministry, from water baptism to baptism with the Spirit, was dramatized in the River Jordan: "And when Jesus was baptized, he went up immediately from the water, and behold, the heavens were opened and he saw the Spirit of God descending like a dove, and alighting on him; and lo, a voice from heaven, saying, 'This is my beloved Son, with whom I am well pleased' " (Matt. 3:16–17). In the waters of baptism Jesus received the Spirit of God, and the transition to a new age began.

What Jesus did throughout his earthly ministry, he did in the power of the Spirit. I can hear your question now: Jesus was God, God from all eternity; why did he need the Holy Spirit's power? A good question, one that needs to be asked and answered. The answer is found in the meaning of Christmas. When God's Son took on human nature as a baby, he set aside the use of his divine power. He *emptied himself* is the way Paul put it (Phil. 2:7). So wholly did he identify with our human experience that he refused to use the godly power that had been his from all eternity. Mind you, he did not cease to be God. God *is*. God's deity is eternal, unchangeable. God cannot *not* be God. But Jesus humbled himself so completely when he took on human flesh, that he determined to depend on the power of his Father and of the Holy Spirit, rather than on his *own* power.

This dependence on God's Spirit is pictured vividly in that baptismal scene, a scene which John the Baptist himself described: "I saw the Spirit descend as a dove from heaven, and it remained on him" (John 1:32). The Spirit of God was present with man in a new way. The works that Jesus did, the words that Jesus said, the love that Jesus showed, the power that Jesus revealed were all possible because God the Spirit was with him and in him. A new way of life—eternal life—was opened for mankind.

The World-wide Application

In that great day of transition, witnessed by the crowds that lined the banks of the Jordan, John promised that Jesus would bring the greater baptism, the baptism of the Holy Spirit. This promise was fulfilled on the day of Pentecost when the Spirit of God was given to the Church. We know this from Jesus' own words: "To them [his disciples] he presented himself alive after his passion by many proofs, appearing to them during forty days, and speaking of the kingdom of God. And while staying with them he charged them not to depart from Jerusalem, but to wait for the promise of the Father, which, he said, 'you heard from me, for John baptized with water, but before many days you shall be baptized with the Holy Spirit'" (Acts 1:3–5).

In his magnificent sermon at Pentecost, Peter explained how Jesus had kept his promise: "Being therefore exalted at the right hand of God, and having received from the Father the promise of the Holy Spirit, he has poured out this which you see and hear" (Acts 2:33).

The incarnate Lord who had lived, died, and risen again through the power of God's Spirit was now pouring out on his fledgling Church—one hundred twenty faithful believers —the same Spirit that came upon him at his baptism. Jesus' ministry began with a baptism; the Church's mission began the same way.

Now the way was paved for a world-wide application of the Spirit's ministry. Not just Jesus was God's Spirit-baptized man, but his whole body was to enter into that baptism. The hundred and twenty were the first fruits of a whole harvest.

Pentecost was the unrepeatable beginning of the whole process. *Unrepeatable* is the right word. Pentecost happened only once. The Church had one beginning, not many, just as Jesus had one incarnation, one crucifixion, one resurrection, one ascension. In the timetable of God's kingdom there was one outpouring of the Spirit, one baptism, that drew Christ's people together and glued them into a cluster called the Church.

To be sure, the Church has expanded and been added to. But there is only one Church, and it had one beginning. Every new conversion is an addition to what began back there. Peter opened the way for these additions when he gave to outsiders the first invitation the newborn Church had ever extended: "And Peter said to them, 'Repent, and

be baptized every one of you in the name of Jesus Christ
for the forgiveness of your sins; and you shall receive the
gift of the Holy Spirit. . . .' So those who received his word
were baptized, and there were added that day about three
thousand souls" (Acts 2:38, 41).

That chain reaction of conversion has exploded through
the centuries and across the world. Everyone who repents of
his sins and puts his trust in Jesus Christ as Lord and Savior
becomes a part of Christ's body, the Christian Church, which
circles our globe and reaches clear to heaven, where believers
from past centuries and decades worship at God's throne:
"There is one body and one Spirit, just as you were called
to the one hope that belongs to your call, one Lord, one
faith, one baptism, one God and Father of us all . . ." (Eph.
4:4–6).

It is the baptism of the Spirit that makes us one. Our
unity is a unity not of language or culture, not of liturgical
form or doctrinal details, but of the Spirit. Whoever truly
confesses the Lord Jesus Christ has the Spirit of God and by
that Spirit is tied to every other believer: "For just as the
body [the *human* body, that is] is one and has many members, and all the members of the body, though many, are
one body, so it is with Christ. For by one Spirit we were
all baptized into one body—Jews or Greeks, slaves or free—
and all were made to drink of one Spirit" (1 Cor. 12:12–13).
The unity of the Church is the result of the baptism of the
Spirit. God himself, God the Holy Spirit, takes each new
believer and immerses him in Christ's body, makes him a
full member of Christ's Church.

The *great transition*, then, began in the great days by the
banks of Jordan, when Jesus Christ's baptism trumpeted the
beginning of a new age, an age when men would know God
and serve each other in the freedom that only the forgiven
can know. This transition was given *world-wide application*
at Pentecost when the one hundred twenty added to their
number the three thousand from all over Caesar's empire.
This world-wide application became personalized when you

and I welcomed Jesus as Savior and were baptized into his body by his Spirit.

Special outpourings of the Spirit there may be on groups and individuals, outpourings of great power and blessing. *Anointings* we should call these, and we should rejoice if God touches us in this way. But the *baptism* of the Spirit is not just another of these anointings, it is the splendid beginning, the grand entry into God's family, for whom there can only be one Lord, one faith, one baptism.

Prayer: Holy Father, what a joy to know that we belong to Christ and to one another. Thank you for sending your Holy Spirit to make this possible. Teach us to live day by day in the joy of that one baptism, through Jesus Christ our Lord. Amen.

3. The Spirit Makes Us New

Remind them to be submissive to rulers and authorities, to be obedient, to be ready for any honest work, to speak evil of no one, to avoid quarreling, to be gentle, and to show perfect courtesy toward all men. For we ourselves were once foolish, disobedient, led astray, slaves to various passions and pleasures, passing our days in malice and envy, hated by men and hating one another; but when the goodness and loving kindness of God our Savior appeared, he saved us, not because of deeds done by us in righteousness, but in virtue of his own mercy, by the washing of regeneration and renewal in the Holy Spirit, which he poured out upon us richly through Jesus Christ our Savior, so that we might be justified by his grace and become heirs in hope of eternal life (Titus 3:1–7).

I could scarcely believe my ears. She looked like an intelligent, attractive woman. I knew her to be a responsible public servant, dedicated to the political party in which she held office. But I could not believe I was hearing her correctly.

The discussion had started out on the subject of public education. After much debate as to what schools should or should not do for students, especially for students from disadvantaged homes, we finally got around to the subject of prayer in the public schools. I think that she was shocked when I replied that to me prayer was too important to be trusted to the public school teachers. I told her that I believed in prayer to the God who is Father, Son, and Holy Spirit and was not interested in any other kind of prayer. Especially in a state like California with its conglomeration of cultures and its kaleidoscope of religions, prayer in our schools—that is, *meaningful* prayer—would be impossible.

It was her next statement that I found incredible: "Well, a little religion would do these kids some good!" I suppose I almost stammered my reply: "A little religion? What you don't realize is that to me religion is a life and death matter. It's heaven or hell. There is no such thing as a *little* religion that will do anybody any good."

It was not to inject a little religion into human life that Jesus came. The Greco-Roman world twenty centuries ago was soil at least as fertile for religious variety as is California's today. More religion was not needed.

Greek and Roman mythology enjoyed a widespread influence. Every major city had its temples and shrines. Holy days and festive celebrations were part of the common life in every country. The names of the deities and the exact forms of the rituals may have varied from Babylon to Byblos to Alexandria to Ephesus to Athens to Corinth to Pompeii to Spain, but the essentials were the same: many gods and goddesses, each with specific functions, each open to appeasement or manipulation by sacrifice and magic. A haunted, fearful world it was, full of superstition and witchcraft.

No wonder the Jewish faith stood out like a lighthouse in the midst of that darkness. One God who directed the course of history and controlled the forces of nature, one God who had liberated an enslaved people and made them his own, one God who had given his people a magnificent code of law and established for them a splendid system of worship—this was the God the Jews worshiped in their better moments and the better Jews worshiped at every moment.

Religion there was plenty of, whether in the pagan Gentile forms or in the Jewish form with its background of supernatural revelation, but Jesus said that this was not enough. And he said it to one of the distinguished religious leaders of the day.

Nicodemus was a Pharisee, learned in the law, loyal to his faith, honored by his people. Jesus told him none of this was enough: "Truly, truly, I say to you, unless one is born anew, he cannot see the kingdom of God. . . . Truly, truly, I say to you, unless one is born of water and the Spirit, he cannot enter the kingdom of God. . . . The wind blows where it wills, and you hear the sound of it, but you do not know whence it comes or whither it goes; so it is with every one who is born of the Spirit" (John 3:3, 5, 8). Not religions, even the best of them, but a new birth, a birth brought about by God's Spirit, was what God demanded—and provided.

A thorough, radical, dramatic change is what man—every man—needed, and still needs. Through God's Holy Spirit this change is possible, possible as he calls lost men, renews their lives, and assures them of their new kinship to God.

The Spirit Calls

Some changes we can bring by sheer resolution. Students who were earning C grades in the first year at college have worked their way up to A by study, concentration, and perhaps learning how to outguess their professors. By discipline women have slimmed down from 240 to 120 pounds, and men have conquered enslaving habits like alcohol or gambling. By dedication athletes of average ability have achieved superior performance, and businessmen of mediocre talent have risen to the top.

Resolution can take us a long way in many areas of life. But the drastic change that Jesus confronted Nicodemus with takes more than resolution.

Our basic problem is beyond the reach of our own will. With many of us our problem lies so deep that we don't recognize it as a problem. Like a mysterious tropical disease it sends its bacteria throughout our whole bloodstream and yet leaves us unaware of its presence. When its symptoms finally surface and we discover how bad off we are, we lack the power to cure ourselves.

A little religion is not enough. Neither is a lot of resolution. No one *comes* to God, in the true sense of that term, unless God calls him. What Paul said to the church of Corinth applies to all of us: "To the church of God which is at Corinth, to those sanctified in Christ Jesus, called to be saints together with all those who in every place call on the name of our Lord Jesus Christ, both their Lord and ours." To these Christians called by God and calling on the name of Christ, Paul extends his blessing: "Grace to you and peace from God our Father and the Lord Jesus Christ" (1 Cor. 1:2–3).

"Called to be saints"—that phrase is key. It implies God's initiative. He it is—God the Holy Spirit—who takes the lead. We do not really call on God until he calls on us. Too sick to call for help, too sick to know how sick we are, we cannot heal ourselves. God's Spirit begins to call us. He may use the preaching of the gospel—perhaps he is speaking to you right now. He may use a verse or a story from the Scriptures. He may use the loving deeds and words of a friend. He may use our failure, loneliness, hardship, despair.

How he does it may vary, but there will be no permanent change without his call.

> 'Twas grace that taught my heart to fear,
> And grace my fears relieved.

Those lines from *Amazing Grace* capture my point. We do not turn to God until he comes after us. He, by his Spirit, probes to the depths of our problem—our sinful rebellion, our arrogant smugness, our subtle selfishness—and tells us that we need to change.

The Spirit Renews

It is only after the Spirit calls us that we begin to know how serious our problems were. Paul describes our pre-Christian days to Titus this way: "For we ourselves were once foolish, disobedient, led astray, slaves to various passions and pleasures, passing our days in malice and envy, hated by men and hating one another" (Titus 3:3). That is not the kind of inscription that we would want on our tombstones. But it has an uncomfortable accuracy to it.

To deal with problems this deep—foolishness, disobedience, envy, malice, lust, hatred—the Spirit of God does more than call us; he renews us. Paul describes how this happens in one of his most powerful paragraphs: "But when the goodness and loving kindness of God our Savior appeared, he saved us, not because of deeds done by us in righteousness, but in virtue of his own mercy, by the washing of regeneration and renewal in the Holy Spirit, which he poured out upon us richly through Jesus Christ our Savior, so that we might be justified by his grace and become heirs in hope of eternal life." Then realizing what an astounding statement he has just made, Paul underlines it with the words, "The saying is sure" (Titus 3:4–8).

The triune God is at work in our salvation. So central to God's program for the world is the salvation of his people that the three persons of the Trinity—Father, Son, Holy Spirit—engage themselves in this task. God the Father, out of the goodness of his love, has made our healing possible. To do so he has given us his Holy Spirit to bring about the needed changes in us, changes which are only possible because of Jesus' death and resurrection. In a massive conspiracy of grace Father, Son, and Spirit have plotted together to turn our lives around.

We must not miss the Spirit's special role. "By the washing of regeneration and renewal in the Holy Spirit" is Paul's description of it. Thorough cleansing, total renewal—these are our needs. We are unclean and defiled by our sin; we are wasting away, destined for decay because of our rebellion.

Then God's Spirit goes to work. Because he is God he knows what our problems are and what to do about them. Because he is God he can create a new kind of life within us. The same Spirit of God that moved over the face of the waters to start creation on its course is present now to breathe his new creation into us. The very life of God is struggling with our old bitter, lonely, angry life and seeking to bring change.

A fresh start, a new hope, a rich relationship are the result. Our account with God has been cleared. Our values and motives begin to change. God at work in us leads us to worship him and to care about each other. Renewal, re-creation, new birth—however we describe it, God and God alone brings drastic change, drastic change for good, drastic change that we are incapable of making.

The Spirit Assures

The work of God's Spirit does not end with this change. He calls us when we have not begun to listen. He renews us in the midst of this mortal disease of sin. And he assures us that we belong to God, that a new relationship of love and trust and obedience has begun: "For all who are led by the Spirit of God are sons of God. For you did not receive the spirit of slavery to fall back into fear, but you have received the spirit of sonship. When we cry, 'Abba! Father!' it is the Spirit himself bearing witness with our spirit that we are children of God" (Rom. 8:14–16).

Do you want to know how much we *need* the Spirit's help if our lives are to change, if we are really to know God? Listen to those words. We cannot even lisp God's name, we cannot even call him 'Daddy' unless the Spirit does it for us.

Do you want to know how much we *can count* on God's help? Listen to those words. God himself in the person of his Spirit actually comes to dwell in us, to make us new, to mold our thoughts, bend our wills, shape our ways. And he even gives us the words to call God 'Father.'

"A little religion is what those children need," the woman told me. Not at all. "A lot of determination will change the world," some optimists believe. Don't bet on it. "You must, you can be born again," Jesus both commanded and promised. The Holy Spirit has fulfilled that promise and enabled that commandment to be obeyed in scores of millions of persons throughout the world. Including me. And, I hope, you.

 Prayer: It is your work of change we have just heard about, O God, Father, Son, Holy Spirit. It is your work of change we have experienced. Keep working in us and in others all around us. For Jesus' sake. Amen.

4. The Spirit
Is God's Seal on His People

Blessed be the God and Father of our Lord Jesus Christ,
who has blessed us in Christ with every spiritual blessing in
the heavenly places, even as he chose us in him before the
foundation of the world, that we should be holy and blame-
less before him. He destined us in love to be his sons through
Jesus Christ, according to the purpose of his will, to the
praise of his glorious grace which he freely bestowed on us
in the Beloved. In him we have redemption through his blood,
the forgiveness of our trespasses, according to the riches of
his grace which he lavished upon us. For he has made known
to us in all wisdom and insight the mystery of his will, ac-
cording to his purpose which he set forth in Christ as a plan
for the fulness of time, to unite all things in him, things in
heaven and things on earth.

In him, according to the purpose of him who accomplishes
all things according to the counsel of his will, we who first
hoped in Christ have been destined and appointed to live for
the praise of his glory. In him you also, who have heard the
word of truth, the gospel of your salvation, and have be-
lieved in him, were sealed with the promised Holy Spirit,
which is the guarantee of our inheritance until we acquire
possession of it, to the praise of his glory (Eph. 1:3–14).

"What does it really mean—this engagement ring?" What
kind of an answer would you get if you put that question to a
bright-eyed couple who had just announced their betrothal?

If they were fully aware of what they were doing (or at
least as aware as a couple can be when their minds are in-
toxicated with emotion), their answer might run like this:
"This ring is a sign and a seal of our commitment to each
other. It means that we have pledged our love and loyalty to

each other for life. Not that we can enjoy each other to the full just yet. That will come at marriage. But by this ring we attest to all who know us that we are reserved for each other. It is a token of a day that is coming, when our love and our relationship will be complete."

Happy is the marriage that can begin with this kind of mature commitment. The girl who receives an engagement ring on these terms is constantly reminded that she belongs to another. She values and treasures this seal because it symbolizes one of the most important decisions she has ever made; it represents a relationship second in significance only to her relationship with God. She may tie a string around her finger to remind her of an errand she has to run after work, but a string is too weak, too cheap, too common to remind her of the covenant she has entered into with her sweetheart.

A valuable ring is the way we have chosen to make clear how deeply we value the commitment to marriage. Of course there may be other motives—less worthy ones—which prompt us to buy an expensive ring: A desire to impress others, the hope of an investment that will appreciate, an eye for fine jewelry. But basically what we are saying is that this crucial transaction needs a suitable symbol of its value and durability. And gold set with diamonds is our most effective way of saying this.

When the gold glistens and the diamond sparkles, all who see it are forced to face the binding nature of this freshly pledged relationship. The man at the neighboring desk in the office is told that there are limits to his neighborliness. That lovely girl may work with him, but she belongs to another. The man who gave the ring is reminded as he sees it (or as he makes the payments on it) that his life and love are invested in this one person. He has nothing left to squander on anyone else. And the girl herself proudly holds herself aloof from all flirtation. The seal on her finger binds her to one man's hand, and she never forgets this.

The engagement ring is both a seal of belonging and a promise of better things to come. It says that the couple are definitely committed to each other but that the full depths of that commitment are yet to be explored.

A seal and a promise—that's what an engagement ring is. In a sense God's Holy Spirit can be compared to an engagement ring. He is much more than that as we have seen. He is a person, with all the same traits of personality that the Father and the Son have. He loves, he cares, he comforts, he convicts, he converts, he teaches, he empowers. By his baptism the Spirit linked us to Christ the head of the Church and to every other member of Christ's body. He called us to God when we were heading the other way at breakneck speed. He made our lives new when the corrupting effects of sin had produced irreversible decay. He assured us that we belonged to God by giving us the very words to call him Father.

How can God the Holy Spirit, who has accomplished all this in our lives and more, be compared with an engagement ring? The same way God the Father can be called a shield and Jesus Christ can be called a foundation. Whenever we talk about God we have to use word pictures to describe his nature and his activities. Human language is all we have to work with, even when the subject of our conversation is God. Comparisons, analogies, word pictures are about the best we can do when it comes to describing the indescribable. Happily, God himself has given us the word pictures with which to talk about him. He is infinite; our language is finite. Yet we can still, with his help, talk about God—Father, Son, Spirit—in ways that are effective and accurate. A seal and a promise or guarantee—this is how Paul describes the Holy Spirit. Let's see what he means.

God's Seal Gives Us a Future Hope

Perhaps the place to begin is Ephesians 1:11–14: "In him [Christ], according to the purpose of him who accomplishes all things according to the counsel of his will, we who first hoped in Christ have been destined and appointed to live for the praise of his glory. In him you also, who have heard the word of truth, the gospel of your salvation, and have believed in him, were sealed with the promised Holy Spirit, which is the guarantee of our inheritance until we acquire possession of it, to the praise of his glory."

Here Paul's eye is on the future. Because we have been sealed by the Spirit, we have a future hope. The Spirit of God is God's guarantee that what we have been promised we will indeed inherit. *Our inheritance is guaranteed.* That is one reason for our future hope.

Wealthy people often set up trusts for their children and grandchildren. Cash, stock, or real property is set aside by a legal agreement. The parents or grandparents can no longer sell it or trade it. On the death of the elders or when the young people reach a designated age, the income from the trust flows directly to the young person. He is the heir; the trust is his legally guaranteed inheritance. Ordinarily a bank handles these pledges through its *trust* department. The very name rings with reliability. The officers who handle the money are carefully screened for their judgment and integrity. Their presence is the guarantee that the heirs will receive all that is coming to them.

We are heirs of God; the kingdom of God, with all its power and glory, is our inheritance. In the scrambled circumstances of our living, it is hard to believe that the wonder of God's kingdom will ever be ours. Impoverished by our own sin, defrauded by the sins of others, we have difficulty remembering how wealthy we are. But God's Spirit is with us as a constant reminder of the wealth of righteousness and fellowship that God has in store for us.

Our immortality and resurrection are assured. This is another reason for our future hope. "For we know that if the earthly tent we live in is destroyed, we have a building from God, a house not made with hands, eternal in the heavens. Here indeed we groan, and long to put on our heavenly dwelling, so that by putting it on we may not be found naked. For while we are still in this tent, we sigh with anxiety; not that we would be unclothed, but that we would be further clothed, so that what is mortal may be swallowed up by life. He who has prepared us for this very thing is God, who has given us the Spirit as a guarantee" (2 Cor. 5:1–5). You get Paul's picture. As we move toward death in a body that proves increasingly frail, we long for the full assurance of immortality for our spirits and resurrection for our bodies. We don't want to fade out when our body dissolves to dust. We will last, and our bodies will be resurrected—that's what God promises. And he backs this promise by sending us the Holy Spirit, who puts God's seal upon us and guarantees our future. As he makes us new right now, reprogramming our motives and values, correcting our intuitions and instincts, refreshing our fallen spirits, he is preparing us for fullness of life as perfected persons in resurrected bodies.

Our wholeness is made certain. This too is a reason for our future hope. "And do not grieve the Holy Spirit of God," Paul commanded, "in whom you were sealed for the day of redemption" (Eph. 4:30). The day of redemption is the time when God's entire program will be complete. It is the culmination of all he has intended and accomplished in history. It marks the end of everything that mars his creation—pain, sorrow, fear, death, sin. All human frailties will be overcome, and those who belong to Christ will be what they have longed to be—whole persons, fully redeemed from everything that held them as slaves. Free persons, full persons, whole persons.

The presence of God's Spirit within us makes it certain that all this will happen. The creator God is steadily at work. His project is nothing less than a new creation. We are part of it.

God's Seal Demands a Present Discipline

When God gives us his Spirit as a seal and guarantee, he transforms our future by filling it with hope. But he does more than that. The Christian life has a present tense which looms large along with the future. Ours is not the faith of an escapist. We do not cling to tomorrow by casting loose today.

When God gives us his Spirit as a seal and guarantee, he demands a present discipline. Our lives are being changed right now. The Spirit who resides within us is called the Holy Spirit. Honesty, control of temper, regard for the property of others, diligence in work, graciousness in speech —these are among the virtues to be cultivated. Failure to do so is called *grieving the Holy Spirit*.

God's people are on the way to full redemption. God's seal is upon them. They are betrothed to him. The Holy Spirit is his engagement ring—not only to remind us but to empower us to be different. Knowing what our future will be like gives us the strongest incentive to live differently now.

In a bold phrase Paul urges us to "be imitators of God" (Eph. 5:1). Left on our own we would find this command ridiculous, if not downright dangerous. Who of us knows enough about God to imitate him? Impersonators hold center stage today. Dozens of them, doing imitations of W. C. Fields, Humphrey Bogart, James Stewart, Hubert Humphrey, President Nixon. Carefully they watch each gesture; like cats they pounce on every mannerism; like hawks they seize upon every tendency to lisp or stammer.

But who knows God this well? Who has the power to live like him? You don't. I don't. That's for sure. But the Holy Spirit is God within us, and he will begin to pattern our life after God's. The life of the future can begin to take hold of us right now, when we are sealed, marked off for God, by his Spirit.

In the Old Testament we hear about *the God who is for us*, calling Israel to himself, entering into a binding compact with his people. In the New Testament we hear it announced that *God is with us*. Immanuel is Jesus' name, as he dwells among us and reveals the Father's love and glory. Beyond that, we read that *God is in us*. Through his Spirit, by whom we have been baptized, made new, and sealed, God is doing in us new things—new things of love and power and grace.

Engagement should be a transforming experience to a couple who take their commitment seriously. The ring by which the transaction is sealed is a prophecy of a bright future and an encouragement to a disciplined present. To all who hear and believe Christ's saving word, this is exactly what God's Spirit means. And much more.

Prayer: Father, you have wooed us and won us by your love. Every today has become bright. Thank you for setting your seal upon us and guaranteeing that tomorrow will be even brighter than today. In Jesus' name we pray. Amen.

5. The Spirit Lives within Us

But you are not in the flesh, you are in the Spirit, if the Spirit of God really dwells in you. Any one who does not have the Spirit of Christ does not belong to him. But if Christ is in you, although your bodies are dead because of sin, your spirits are alive because of righteousness. If the Spirit of him who raised Jesus from the dead dwells in you, he who raised Christ Jesus from the dead will give life to your mortal bodies also through his Spirit which dwells in you.

So then, brethren, we are debtors, not to the flesh, to live according to the flesh—for if you live according to the flesh you will die, but if by the Spirit you put to death the deeds of the body you will live. For all who are led by the Spirit of God are sons of God. For you did not receive the spirit of slavery to fall back into fear, but you have received the spirit of sonship. When we cry, "Abba! Father!" it is the Spirit himself bearing witness with our spirit that we are children of God, and if children, then heirs, heirs of God and fellow heirs with Christ, provided we suffer with him in order that we may also be glorified with him (Rom. 8:9–17).

Riveted to our television sets we watched them, watched them walk on the moon. It was the last moon mission for the foreseeable future—Apollo 17—and millions of us were taking another close look at the moon and the amazing men who had made the lonely pilgrimage to its barren surface.

With more padding than hockey players wear, they hopped along the dusty lunar paths. With stronger helmets than football linemen use, they roamed the nooks and crannies of our neighbor planet, snapping their pictures and planting their equipment. Those sturdy spacesuits and those massive helmets were absolutely essential to their well-being.

One of the astronauts was scolded by Mission Control for leaving his sun visor up. He could see more clearly with it up on his head out of his line of vision. But the crew in Houston made him put it down. Unsure of how the sun might affect his face and eyes, they took no chances.

After their work shifts the astronauts had to climb the ladder up to their landing module. There they could shed their helmets and their pressurized suits, and they could eat and sleep. The elaborate outfits, the custom-made helmets, the breathing packs on their backs, the intricately designed cockpit with its tight seals and accurate gages all have one purpose: they allow men to carry something of earth's presence with them into space.

As clever as man is, he cannot live without earth's environment. The pressures, temperatures, atmosphere of the moon are all intolerable to him. He only survives by wrapping himself in a support system that packages earth's environment and carries it with him into space. Made for life on earth, man dare not venture further than he can take earth's presence with him.

Perhaps all this can give us a rough idea of what it means for the Holy Spirit of God to live in God's people. Christ's mission had brought drastic changes in the lives of his followers. When he found them, they were men tied to this world—its values, moods, attitudes, and enterprises. As fishermen, tax collectors, laborers, they had scrounged for a living, struggled to raise their families, pondered the meaning of life. Then Jesus found them and called them. His attitudes and values became theirs. He drafted them to become part of his mission, and he gave them a new and true picture of God as heavenly Father.

Sons of the heavenly Father they became. And with this sonship they gained a new citizenship. Heaven, where God's will is done, is the kingdom to which they pledged their allegiance. As long as Jesus was with them, their new life was sustained by his words, his power, his example, his love.

He kept them in touch with the Father in heaven. He instructed them daily in the duties of their sonship, in the responsibilities of their citizenship.

When Jesus began to talk about leaving, the question understandably arose as to how this support and this instruction could continue. Who would bring the very presence of heaven to them in the stifling atmosphere of earth? Here is Jesus' answer: "If you love me, you will keep my commandments. And I will pray the Father, and he will give you another Counselor, to be with you for ever, even the Spirit of truth, whom the world cannot receive, because it neither sees him nor knows him; you know him, for he dwells with you, and will be in you" (John 14:15-17).

". . . another Counselor, to be with you for ever . . . he dwells with you, and will be in you." The disciples knew about the Holy Spirit. They were familiar with the prediction of John the Baptist that Jesus would baptize with the Holy Spirit and with fire. Some of them may have been present on the banks of the River Jordan that remarkable day when the Holy Spirit, in the form of a dove, descended on their Messiah. They had heard their Master speak of the Spirit whom the Father would give to those who asked. They had seen the Savior do mighty works in the Spirit's power. The Spirit had been *among* them. Wherever Jesus went, God's Spirit was present. Now they faced a dramatic change. Jesus was going away, and the Holy Spirit was to dwell *in* them.

The Spirit Shows That We Belong to God

The day of Pentecost brought the fulfillment of Jesus' promise. The Holy Spirit came upon the disciples to abide within them. And not only within them, but within all those who by faith belong to God's family.

"But you are not in the flesh, you are in the Spirit, if the Spirit of God really dwells in you. Any one who does not have the Spirit of Christ does not belong to him" (Romans

8:9). The Spirit shows that we belong to God. Our alienation from him is over; our estrangement is past.

Man's rebellion put a gap between him and God. It dug a gulf too wide for man to bridge. The cross where our sin was punished, the resurrection where our death was defeated, Pentecost where God's Spirit was sent to the Church—these mighty acts of God form a bridge by which man can come back to him, a bridge built from God's side.

The cross on which Jesus died demonstrates how serious our rebellion was. God sent his Son to quell our insurrection. It cost him his life to do it. But a just and lasting peace became possible.

The empty tomb from which Christ came out alive demonstrates how great God's victory was. The last, worst, most permanent enemy of man was devastated, done in. New life was possible, free from the domination of sin and the fear of death.

The rushing wind and fiery tongues of Pentecost demonstrate God's presence among us. The new life which death and resurrection made possible was to be sustained and deepened by God himself. He was to be present with all who belonged to him. His very presence was the badge of their belonging.

This is not just a return to the Garden—this forgiveness of sin, this power over death, this indwelling presence of God. It is more than Eden ever dreamed of. In that garden at the beginning, God came at the cool of the day and talked with man. Now he actually lives within men and women, those who have hung their hopes on Jesus Christ. In that garden man knew only the grace of God's creation—the beauty and bounty of nature. Now man has tasted of the fruit of God's forgiveness, the sweetest human experience possible. In that garden man faced only the vague threat of his dying. Now, having counted into the millions the coffins of his forerunners and his friends, he rejoices in death's downfall. He belongs to God. God's presence is in him. He would not trade that for a hundred Edens.

The Spirit Makes Us Entirely New

God's presence brings changes. The Spirit is not just a guest who dwells in our lives, sensitive to our habits, abiding by our schedules. He is more a manager than a guest. When he comes, he takes charge. What else could God the Holy Spirit do?

As manager, one of his chief tasks is renovation, restoration, renewal. He has moved into a personality where sin and death have been in charge. Like a wicked partnership they have used us to their own advantage, and in our stubbornness and foolishness we have given them full cooperation.

The Holy Spirit sets out to evict sin and death, and to undo their terrible damage. Our spirits need help badly. They have been abused to the point of death by our rebellion. Cut off from the God who is Spirit they have shriveled, withered, decayed, died. The worship of God and the fellowship with him for which our spirits were made have been impossible. Like branches cruelly severed from the vine they have perished.

But the presence of Christ brings them back to life. "But if Christ is in you, although your bodies are dead because of sin, your spirits are alive because of righteousness" (Rom. 8:10). The Spirit of God, who can also be called the Spirit of Christ, because he does the work of both the Father and the Son, brings new life to our spirits. The impact of sin is countered by the righteousness of Christ. What we could not do—keep God's law—Christ has done for us. What we could not achieve—true love and perfect worship—Christ has accomplished in our place. As we stake our lives on what he has done, our spirits are brought to life by Christ's Spirit. Christ's righteousness is shared with us, who deserved it not at all. And new life begins.

But the new life does not limit itself to our spirits. Our bodies are doomed to decay. The Holy Spirit, God's great manager within us, goes to work on them as well. "If the

Spirit of him who raised Jesus from the dead dwells in you, he who raised Christ Jesus from the dead will give life to your mortal bodies also through his Spirit which dwells in you" (Rom. 8:11).

Our bodies, inching their way toward certain death, are being readied for resurrection. The twitches and tweaks, ticks and jerks, quivers and wobbles, aches and shakes are not the last word. Resurrection is. The Spirit who lives within all of those who truly call Christ by name will see to it that final restoration takes place in the days to come. The same God who raised Jesus has sent his Spirit to make our resurrection possible.

Better than a heart transplant this is. Skilled surgeons may lengthen life a couple of months or even a year by planting a new heart within a person. But eventually both heart and body will die. God's Spirit brings our spirits to life forever and promises new bodies as well. That's real restoration!

The Spirit Strengthens Us for Moral Living

It is a restoration that changes our lives right now. *God's Spirit links us to Christ* as members of a body are linked to its head. As a member of Christ's body, I am strengthened by the Holy Spirit to live a moral life. Paul put a blunt question to the Corinthians: "Shall I therefore take the members of Christ and make them members of a prostitute? . . . he who is united to the Lord becomes one spirit with him. Shun immorality" (1 Cor. 6:15, 17, 18).

God's Spirit makes a temple of our bodies. This is another way that the Holy Spirit strengthens us for moral living. Our lives are changed, made new. We are no longer brothels of immorality, theaters for entertainment, casinos for gambling, gymnasiums for recreation, libraries for research, offices for commerce. We are temples. God lives within. And all that we do is hallowed by his presence.

The world is full of fine church buildings. Chartres with its exquisite glass, Notre Dame with its sturdy buttresses, Salisbury with its spire of flawless proportions. But the real masterpieces of church architecture are you, me, our friends, our brothers and sisters in every nation, whose lives are linked to Christ by the Spirit, whose bodies have become temples so valuable that only Christ's blood could buy them. Are you among them? God wants your body, your person, as his home. And when you take him in, he brings with him something of the very atmosphere of heaven.

Prayer: Father, we remember one of the most important promises your Son ever made: "If a man loves me, he will keep my word, and my Father will love him, and we will come to him and make our home with him" (John 14:23). Continue to do your great work, making that promise come true in each one of us. For Jesus' sake. Amen.

6. The Spirit Gives Us Power

So when they had come together, they asked him, "Lord, will you at this time restore the kingdom to Israel?" He said to them, "It is not for you to know times or seasons which the Father has fixed by his own authority. But you shall receive power when the Holy Spirit has come upon you; and you shall be my witnesses in Jerusalem and in all Judea and Samaria and to the end of the earth." And when he had said this, as they were looking on, he was lifted up, and a cloud took him out of their sight. And while they were gazing into heaven as he went, behold, two men stood by them in white robes, and said, "Men of Galilee, why do you stand looking into heaven? This Jesus, who was taken up from you into heaven, will come in the same way as you saw him go into heaven" (Acts 1:6–11).

When *power* is mentioned, what picture comes to your mind? The massive turbines that generate electricity in our great dams of western America—Grand Coulee, Bonneville, Hoover? Twirling with energy these turbines generate enough electricity to keep huge factories humming and to set sprawling cities ablaze with light. That's power.

Or you may think of the atomic energy seen in mushroom cloud explosions that have shaken deserts in Nevada and New Mexico and have leveled cities in Japan. Submarines and ships powered with this energy plow through heavy seas months at a time without refueling. In the shielded laboratories of our universities enough energy is generated to smash the smallest, toughest atoms into their tiny parts. That's power.

When I think of power in nature the Amazon River probably holds first place in my thought. Many of the missionaries that listen to our broadcast live along its 14,000 miles of navigable waterways. They could describe its power better than I. They know it firsthand.

A recent article in the *National Geographic* (October 1972) gave some statistics about the Amazon River that are almost incredible. Among rivers, the Amazon is in a class by itself. Its volume of water is greater than the total of the eight other largest rivers on earth. We know how vast the Nile is and the way in which all of Egypt has depended on its magnificent flooding for irrigation from time immemorial. Yet the Amazon at its mouth discharges sixty times as much water as the Nile. Each day the Amazon is running full it spews into the Atlantic eight trillion gallons. That colossal figure may not mean much to us unless we know that it amounts to two hundred times the total volume that all the cities in the United States use daily. Or, to put it another way, the Amazon discharges every day enough water to supply the total United States need for industry, agriculture, and electrical energy twenty times over. That's power.

As Christians we know that there is more to the subject of power than humming turbines, exploding atoms, and roaring rivers. In a sense all of these are evidences of God's power. Whence come the electrons that flow through the ribbons of cable to light our cities? Whence comes the energy that can rearrange the very structure of matter in nuclear reactions? Whence comes the water that carves canyons in the landscape and drives relentlessly toward the sea? The Christian knows. No one but God can create matter, energy, water. No one but God has the raw power to reshape the contours of our planet. Man may harness and distribute the power. But its true source is God.

And God has other kinds of power. Not so readily apparent, not so obviously striking, not so constantly visible, but *power*—divine power—nonetheless. The power of the Holy Spirit at work among Christ's people is a good example. It is power like a mighty river that can quench the spiritual thirst of the whole world. Jesus himself described it this way. It was on the last day of the feast (the Feast of Tabernacles which Jesus attended in Jerusalem) that Jesus proclaimed, "If any one thirst, let him come to me and drink. He who believes in me, as the scripture has said, 'Out of his heart shall flow rivers of living water.'" Lest there be any misunderstanding of Jesus' words, John the apostle tells us what they mean. "Now this he said about the Spirit, which those who believed in him were to receive; for as yet the Spirit had not been given, because Jesus was not yet glorified" (John 7:37–39).

The person who believes is to have the Spirit's own power within him flowing like a mighty river. The Day of Pentecost was, of course, the beginning of this. The infant Church, overwhelmed by its task of carrying out the Master's orders, was given God's own power to do so. The glorified Christ—honored by God for completing his mission in dying, rising, ascending—fulfilled his promise and sent the rivers of water to provide refreshment and power for his Church in its world-wide mission.

Power for Effective Witness

That promise which he had given earlier in his ministry he repeated after his resurrection, just before he left his followers to return to the Father. Luke tells the story in some detail. "So when they [i.e., the apostles] had come together, they asked him, 'Lord, will you at this time restore the kingdom to Israel?' He said to them, 'It is not for you to know times or seasons which the Father has fixed by his own authority. But you shall receive power when the Holy Spirit has come upon you; and you shall be my witnesses in Jerusalem and in all Judea and Samaria and to the end of the earth'" (Acts 1:6–8).

Power for effective witness—this is one of the Holy Spirit's great gifts. Just how the Spirit's power works in effective witness is one of those mysteries of God which are beyond our reach. But the Scriptures and our own experience give us clues that may shed some light on the matter.

Conviction in the face of doubt is one thing the power of God's Spirit gives us. To his friends at Rome Paul wrote: "For I am not ashamed of the gospel: it is the power of God for salvation to every one who has faith, to the Jew first and also to the Greek" (Rom. 1:16). No one can witness effectively who is not convinced that the gospel really works. Doubt dampens the fires of witness until they burn so low that no one can see them. What the Spirit does is to reassure us that God can and will change lives. He reminds us of what Christ has done for us. In other words he refuels our faith by the oil of his own presence within. He continues to convince us that Jesus is our powerful Lord and our loving Savior. With this conviction, we have the strength to reach out to others.

Courage in the midst of opposition is another powerful gift of God's Spirit to help us as we share our faith with others. Think of Stephen, the first martyr, the first witness to die for his faith. By the way, witness and *martyr* mean the same thing in the New Testament, where the Greek word for witness is martyr. To witness is to risk your life for the truth of what you believe. This Stephen did. Though he knew it meant death, he did not bury the light of his witness; he let it burn brightly in the midst of opposition. And he added to the strength of his testimony by praying for his enemies. An amazing picture of the courage which God's Spirit can give.

Confidence in every situation is yet another help the Spirit gives. In his promise, Jesus specifically mentioned the expanding arena within which Christian witness would be displayed. Jerusalem, the home base where both cordial friends and hostile enemies lived, was to receive its witness. So were Judea and Samaria, the neighboring territories that were so frequently at odds with each other. In fact, no part of the world was to be cheated of the privilege of hearing and believing. God was not a regional God; Christ was not a local hero; the gospel was not a provincial message. The Spirit could go anywhere that believers could go; he would do his work anywhere that people lived; he could translate the

Christian message into any language and culture under the sun.

Concern for all kinds of people is one of our deepest needs. This, too, the Spirit gives us as part of his power for effective witness. Not only Stephen, who asked forgiveness for his enemies, but Paul demonstrated this. "For I could wish that I myself were accursed and cut off from Christ for the sake of my brethren, my kinsmen by race" (Rom. 9:3). So great was his concern, he was willing to be lost himself if that were the only way they could be saved. It is difficult for us to reach people in Christ's name, unless they feel that we care about them. A Canadian woman, a nurse, told me about an experience she had in Labrador. An old fisherman came to her with a massive toothache. When he opened his mouth, she almost threw up. Disease, decay, filth covered almost every tooth. She recoiled at first and snatched her hand back. Then she thought of what the grace of Christ had done for her foul corruption. Into that vile mouth went her· clean hand. The Holy Spirit gave her a powerful concern even for a repulsive old fisherman.

Power for Christian Endurance

We cannot witness effectively without the Spirit's power. Nor can we keep steady in our Christian life. We are not gliders whom the Spirit helps get off the ground so that we can soar on our own. We are more like airplanes whose flight depends on a constant flow of power. We are closer to turbines than tops. The Spirit is not God's string that sets us spinning; he is God's river that ever flows to provide our power.

To the Galatians Paul spoke sharply about this. "Are you so foolish? Having begun with the Spirit, are you now ending with the flesh?" (Gal. 3:3). Tempted to quit, discouraged by our failures, fearful of the obstacles life sends our way, we tend to fall back into our old pre-Christian patterns. We walk by sight, not faith. Working out our own solutions takes the place of our trusting in God. We begin to rely on something besides the Spirit's power.

Yet only he can give power for Christian endurance. There is no greater frustration than trying to live on Christ's terms without Christ's power. To do his will, to follow his way, to obey his word takes his help. That's all there is to it.

Howie was the young son of friends of mine. As he went off to school for the very first time, his mother prayed with him at the doorway. She asked God to give him strength and help for his new venture. For three days she did this. On the fourth day, she again suggested prayer. Howie, confident because of his successes the past three days, answered, "No, thanks. I'd like to try it on my own." We share his temptation. We must not give in. Like a glorious river, God's Spirit gives us power for Christian endurance.

Power for Holy Living

One other word needs to be said about the Spirit's power. He helps us witness effectively; he gives us the strength we need to endure. And more, he enables us to live holy lives. "For this is the will of God, your sanctification: that you abstain from immorality" (1 Thess. 4:3). This was the stern advice Paul gave to the new believers in Thessalonica. Carefully he argued that they should heed the will of God, that they should respect a neighbor's right by not touching his wife, and that they should bear in mind the dangers of God's judgment.

But it is to the climax of his argument that I want to point: "For God has not called us for uncleanness, but in holiness. Therefore whoever disregards this, disregards not man but God, who gives his Holy Spirit to you" (1 Thess. 4:7–8). Underline *Holy* in this clause. The Spirit God gives is the *Holy* Spirit. He has power to make us holy in what we do and how we do it.

Before Jesus made his promise of the Spirit, his disciples had asked about the kingdom. When would it be restored?

He would not tell them when. But he did tell them how. Where the Holy Spirit works, there Christ's kingdom is present. As the Spirit gives power to our witness, Christ's kingdom is expanded. As the Spirit gives power for Christian endurance, Christ's kingdom is strengthened. As the Spirit gives power for holy living, Christ's kingdom is perfected.

With Amazon-like power, and more, God's Spirit is on the move. Go with him. You will be amazed at what happens.

Prayer: Father, in the midst of our lack of power you have come to us. Our lips are stuck shut until your Spirit gives them power to celebrate the Savior's name. Our faith will wobble and falter unless you keep it constant. Our lives will reek of corruption, if your Spirit does not keep them fragrant. Make us faithful witnesses, for Jesus' sake. Amen.

7. The Spirit Convicts the World of Sin

"I have said all this to you to keep you from falling away. They will put you out of the synagogues; indeed, the hour is coming when whoever kills you will think he is offering service to God. And they will do this because they have not known the Father, nor me. But I have said these things to you, that when their hour comes you may remember that I told you of them.

"I did not say these things to you from the beginning, because I was with you. But now I am going to him who sent me; yet none of you asks me, 'Where are you going?' But because I have said these things to you, sorrow has filled your hearts. Nevertheless I tell you the truth: it is to your advantage that I go away, for if I do not go away, the Counselor will not come to you; but if I go, I will send him to you. And when he comes, he will convince the world of sin and of righteousness and of judgment: of sin, because they do not believe in me; of righteousness, because I go to the Father, and you will see me no more; of judgment, because the ruler of this world is judged" (John 16:1–11).

It looked as if Christ had failed. He came as light into the world, but the world preferred its darkness. He came as bread from heaven, but the world continued to eat its earthly chaff and straw. He came as living water, but the world still tried to quench its thirst at its own stagnant cistern.

Men could easily brand Christ a failure. He was sent as proof that God loved the world. Yet the people in the world refused to look at the evidence. Or when they did, they rejected it as unconvincing. "If God really loved us, we would not suffer as we do," they held. "This talk of God's love is sharply contradicted by the disease that ravages our young, by the hopelessness that plagues our aged, by the poverty and oppression that grind us all. Who can talk of love when he has to scrounge for bread? Who can hear of care when he is taxed to the bone by foreign oppressors?"

"Besides," the men of Jesus' day might have gone on, "our tradition tells us of God's love. As we keep his law he blesses us with his love. Why do we need a carpenter from Nazareth to show us what we already know from our holy books? Does he know more than our learned rabbis? Is he a better teacher than our distinguished priests and scribes?

"His claims seem brash, presumptuous. He promises an abundant life and a true knowledge of God to those who follow him, and to them alone. That's too exclusive a doctrine for us and too demanding.

"Yet his teaching is so attractive, his manner so winsome, his power so evident that we can't ignore him. He must be resisted, exposed, put away. He who purports to be the savior of the world must be labeled an arch-enemy. And in God's name his followers, that deluded crew of unlearned peasants, must be wiped out." So said some of the wiser, more powerful of Jesus' countrymen and their Roman henchmen with whom they made common cause in their hatred of Jesus.

It looked as if Christ had failed. He who came to declare God's love for the world was received by a comparative handful of men and women, none of them powerful, none distinguished. Furthermore, far from drawing the positive response of faith and obedience that he sought, he had succeeded only in building up a volume of hostility that threatened to drown him and to swamp his followers.

This appearance of failure Jesus faced squarely with his loved ones. "I have said all this to you to keep you from falling away. They will put you out of the synagogues; indeed, the hour is coming when whoever kills you will think he is offering service to God. And they will do this because they have not known the Father, nor me. But I have said these things to you, that when their hour comes you may remember that I told you of them" (John 16:1-3).

Persecution was on the way. The same Book of Acts that tells how Christ's promises were fulfilled when he sent the Spirit at Pentecost tells how these dire predictions were fulfilled in the imprisonment of Peter and the brutal deaths of Stephen and James.

Jesus' answer to this persecution is what holds our attention here. He repeated his promise to send the Spirit as an Advocate, an influential friend to plead their cause in court. The Spirit would give them the same strength to face opposition that they felt when Jesus was with them. And more than that, he would give them wisdom in how to answer their enemies. "Beware of men; for they will deliver you up to councils, and flog you in their synagogues, and you will be dragged before governors and kings for my sake, to bear testimony before them and the Gentiles. When they deliver you up, do not be anxious how you are to speak or what you are to say; for what you are to say will be given to you in that hour; for it is not you who speak, but the Spirit of your Father speaking through you" (Matt. 10:17–20).

Strength to face the world at its most hostile—this Jesus promised. You can guess how reassuring this was to the disciples. You can almost hear them sigh in relief. But then you can also hear them gasp in surprise as Jesus went on to promise something greater—not only strength to face the world at its most hostile but also power to change the world at its most sinful: "And when he comes [i.e., the Holy Spirit], he will convince the world of sin and of righteousness and of judgment" (John 16:8).

Jesus was leaving the world; he was not abandoning it. It only *looked* as if he had failed. He had a master plan to fulfill his purposes. The world's hostility played into his master plan. He would use it to test the mettle of his men; he would use it to sharpen the contrast between his kingdom of worship and love, and Satan's kingdom of idolatry and hate.

Jesus was leaving the world, but he was not through with it. His plan to share his Father's love with the people of the world was yet to be carried out. This was the work of the

Holy Spirit—not just to encourage the disciples, but through them to change the world.

To do this the Spirit had to *convict* the world and to *convince* the world of its mistakes. The Greek word carries both meanings—convict and convince. The Spirit declares the world guilty. His verdict is clear and final. Against it there is no appeal. As the prosecuting attorney reviewing the sins of men, he has a closed case. And he presses it home.

But this is not enough. Condemnation is not Christ's main purpose. Salvation is. When the Holy Spirit convicts the world, he works also to convince them that the verdict is right. They must agree with that verdict and want to be changed. That's what the Bible means by repentance.

The Spirit Convinces the World of Sin

On the eve of his death, Jesus considered his work finished. The hour was at hand. He was ready for it. Even eager. It was not only his moment of suffering; it was his moment of glory, his hour of obedience, his time of fulfillment. The next great effort to bring men to understand God's love was to be made by the Spirit, soon to come.

His first task was to convince the world that its basic sin was unbelief. ". . . they do not believe in me" was the simple, direct way that Jesus put it (John 16:9). At first glance, unbelief does not seem such a terrible sin. It goes on among us all the time, and we don't call it sin.

A politician may question the judgment of people who do not vote for him. But he does not call them sinners. A team may question the loyalty of a hometown crowd that boos the mistakes of its own team and cheers the good play of the opposition. But they do not call those who refuse to believe *sinners*.

Yet Jesus did just this. Why? The answer lies in who Jesus is and what God sent him to accomplish. Not to believe in Jesus is to refuse to take God seriously. That is the ultimate sin, the rejection of God's revelation of himself. Idolatry, I suppose you might call this. If one refuses to believe that Jesus is God, it must mean that he believes something or someone else is God. If he does, he is an idolater.

Unbelief in Jesus is *the* sin. It cuts us off from true knowledge of God, and it renders us helpless. We may decide not to believe in a certain politician and do no great harm to ourselves. We may choose not to root for a certain team without any dire consequences. But not to believe in Jesus is the essence of sin. By our unbelief we disdain God's greatest gift and deprive ourselves of any real hope in life.

One crucial task of God's Spirit, then, is to expose the guilt of those who do not believe and to show them how wrong they are. It is hard for anyone to take steps to get well who does not admit that he is ill.

The Spirit Convinces the World of Righteousness

The world fails at another point. It refuses to acknowledge Christ's righteousness. Here again unbelievers show their shortsightedness. They discount God's own evaluation of Jesus. How righteous was Christ? How good? How true in his conduct? How splendid in his relationships? God himself gave the answer: "This is my beloved Son, with whom I am well pleased" (Matt. 3:17).

Who can argue with that? But that's not all. Christ did his work for God so well, he completed it so totally, that he was welcomed back to the side of God in full honor and glory. This is what he means when he announces that the Spirit will convince the world "of righteousness, because I go to the Father, and you will see me no more" (John 16:10).

His work of righteousness was complete. Now it was the Holy Spirit's task to *convict* men of their lack of righteousness and to *convince* them of their *need* for it. Christ's work of righteousness was complete—not only because of his righteous life but because of his righteous death. His *life* carried a consistent quality of righteousness: he did and said right things; he treated people right; he maintained right relationships with friends and foes alike. His *death* was a demonstration of righteousness. It showed how much a righteous God cared about our sins. It made it possible for us to be counted among the righteous, despite our lack of personal righteousness.

Now Christ was to go away. His work was finished. But the Spirit was sent to help us understand that work and apply it. And he begins by showing us the wrongness of our unbelief, and prodding us to seek Christ's righteousness.

The Spirit Convinces the World of Judgment

Jesus' final words about the Spirit's mission in the world show just how serious the situation is. Men and women in the world refuse to believe in Jesus, and they reject the righteousness he demonstrated by his life and provided in his death. The Holy Spirit struggles with them to help them realize this. But more than that, he has to make them know that judgment awaits them if they persist in their unbelief.

As proof of this judgment Jesus pointed to the fate of Satan. The Spirit's job is to convince the world "of judgment, because the ruler of this world is judged" (John 16:11). In his temptation Jesus defeated Satan, who tried to sidetrack him from his mission. In his righteous life Jesus defeated Satan, who used all manner of pressure to break his morale and divert him from his course. In his obedient death Jesus defeated Satan, who tried to persuade him to shun the cross and to leave our sins undealt with. In his resurrection and ascension Jesus defeated Satan, who tried to hold him fast in the clutches of death.

In this running battle Jesus won every contest. The prince of this world, powerful as he is, was no match for the King of heaven. Satan was judged the loser. His final defeat was assured. Let Satan's defeat be a warning to all Satan's followers, Jesus urged. If the captain has gone down, how can his troops expect to stand? If the master has been crushed in defeat, what hope of victory can his servants hold? Part of the work of God's Spirit is to show the foes of Christ that they have lost and their best hope lies in surrender.

From time to time the islands of the Pacific send strange reports to the rest of the world—reports of Japanese soldiers who do not know that World War II is over or who have refused to surrender. Out of fanatical loyalty to their Emperor and his commanders they have kept alive the dream of victory. Unrealistic, foolish, we call them. Their forces went down to defeat long ago. So did Satan's, but millions of people persist in serving him. I hope you are not among them.

From what looked like failure, Christ promised victory. The disciples would endure; their company would expand; their message would change the world. The Holy Spirit made the difference. He still does.

Prayer: Father, use my life to change the world. I know your Spirit is within me, because you have told me so. Help me to live and to speak so that others may know that too. It is easy to retreat from the world; it is easy to be corrupted by the world. Make me part of your program to bring men and women to the truth of Jesus Christ, through whom I pray. Amen.

8. The Spirit Counsels the Church

"If you love me, you will keep my commandments. And I will pray the Father, and he will give you another Counselor, to be with you for ever, even the Spirit of truth, whom the world cannot receive, because it neither sees him nor knows him; you know him, for he dwells with you, and will be in you" (John 14:15–17).

"These things I have spoken to you, while I am still with you. But the Counselor, the Holy Spirit, whom the Father will send in my name, he will teach you all things, and bring to your remembrance all that I have said to you. Peace I leave with you; my peace I give to you; not as the world gives do I give to you. Let not your hearts be troubled, neither let them be afraid. You heard me say to you, 'I go away, and I will come to you.' If you loved me, you would have rejoiced, because I go to the Father; for the Father is greater than I. And now I have told you before it takes place, so that when it does take place, you may believe. I will no longer talk much with you, for the ruler of this world is coming. He has no power over me; but I do as the Father has commanded me, so that the world may know that I love the Father. Rise, let us go hence" (John 14:25–31).

You have watched it happen numbers of times. The policeman in the television drama is informing the arrested person of his rights. His statement goes something like this: "It is my duty to inform you of your rights. You are not obliged to make any statement until you have consulted your lawyer. However, I must warn you that any statement you do make may be held against you. You have the right to call an attorney of your choosing. Or if you prefer, the court will appoint an attorney to represent you. Do you understand these rights of which you have now been duly informed?"

The scene in the TV story usually goes on to show the person arrested telephoning his lawyer to call for help. Most of us would do the same thing, if we were in that position. The law is complex; our rights may prove fragile without someone skilled to defend them.

Skilled should be underlined. As in any profession, some lawyers are more competent than others. Were we in trouble, we would try to get the best—a counselor with fine training, wide experience, solid reputation.

More than that we would hope for an advocate who had great power to persuade. The prosecuting attorney may use every technique available to convince the judge or jury of our guilt. To counter his influence, our lawyer needs to see the issues keenly, to spot the loopholes in the argument and the thin places in the evidence, and then to drive his case home with all the clarity and forcefulness that he can muster. Our welfare is at stake; we want the best help we can get.

There is something else we want from an attorney if we find ourselves in trouble. *Concern*, that's what we want. Perhaps more than anything else we want to believe that the one who represents us in court is concerned for our well-being. He may want to preserve or enhance his reputation by doing a good job in our case. That's understandable. He wants to collect a fee representative of the amount of work he has put in. That's only fair. But down deep you hope he has more than reputation or compensation in mind. You hope he is thinking of you—your rights, your freedom, your future.

You want an experienced, able, well-trained lawyer who is also a friend. With someone like that at your side, your trouble does not become enjoyable. But it may become at least bearable.

Why all this talk about lawyers in a study of the Holy Spirit? Because that is just what the Holy Spirit is—a powerful Advocate for our cause, a Lawyer skilled in dealing with those who oppose us, a firm Friend committed to help us.

When Jesus called the Holy Spirit our Comforter or Coun-

selor, this is what he meant. The comfort the Spirit gives is
not just consolation in our times of sorrow, though he certainly does that. It is help and strength in times when men
oppose or even persecute us.

What the Holy Spirit does for us is so rich and so varied
that no one word is large enough to describe his ministry.
Helper, Strengthener, Comforter, Advocate, Counselor,
Friend—all these and more he is. The term Jesus used was
Paraclete, a Greek word that means something like "one who
is called to your side in order to render help." Though there
is a legal tone to the term, there is more than that. The Spirit
is a lawyer who is also a close friend. He stands by us in all
our troubles because he really cares about us. That is something of what the name *Paraclete* implies.

Perhaps the best way to get at the meaning of the word is
to look at the things the Spirit does for us. In his conversations with the disciples just before the crucifixion, Jesus promised that the Father would send the Holy Spirit. And he did
more than that. He mentioned a number of specific things
that the Spirit, as the *Paraclete*, the Lawyer-Counselor-
Friend, would do. In every crucial area of need, God's Spirit
will give us help. Lack of understanding of God's will and
ways is one of our problems. The Holy Spirit helps us *to
think clearly*. Moral compromise is a constant temptation.
The Holy Spirit helps us to *live purely*. Courage to acknowledge our faith before others is a pressing need. The Holy
Spirit helps us *to witness boldly*.

Helping Us to Think Clearly

True knowledge of God is part of what Christ came to
bring. He showed God's power in what he did; he opened
up God's truth in what he said; he revealed God's love in how
he cared. The impact of his life was overwhelming. He had
worked so mightily, he had spoken so wisely, he had cared so
deeply that his disciples could not possibly understand or
even remember all of it.

Jesus was not about to leave them to their own devices, to abandon them to their own faulty recollections and partial insights. "These things I have spoken to you, while I am still with you. But the Counselor [that's our word *Paraclete*], the Holy Spirit, whom the Father will send in my name, he will teach you all things, and bring to your remembrance all that I have said to you" (John 14:25–26).

Teaching and reminding were two of the Spirit's chief tasks. And they were crucial ones. For three years Jesus had taught the profoundest lessons men had ever heard. Much of what he said the disciples did not really understand. In fact they frequently misunderstood and had to be corrected. They thought his kingdom was a political one, and they vied for positions of power in it. They resisted the thought of his death, thinking it meant defeat for his program. Time and again his words were too deep, his thoughts too high for them to grasp. Yet now that he was leaving, they, who had understood so little, were to be responsible for interpreting his words and deeds to the whole world. No wonder they needed God's Spirit!

Christ left no books behind, no definitive explanations of his program. On the memories and insights of these eleven men (remember Judas had already left) the success of his program was to hinge. They had to have help to think clearly the thoughts of Christ himself.

The Spirit did his job well. The Church expanded; Jews and Gentiles believed the message; the Scriptures were completed. Obviously, some men and women misunderstood the Christian faith. Heretical sects developed in many places; controversies arose which produced sharp tensions in the young Church. But along the way the Spirit did his work, and the faith of the apostles was preserved and passed along from continent to continent, from generation to generation.

And now it has come to us. Their recollections of Jesus and their interpretations of his story have come down to us in the New Testament. What they had earlier misunderstood was made clear to them. What they had been in danger of forgetting was etched in their memories. We have it in writing. And the same Spirit who helped them understand and remember helps us understand and obey. The Holy Spirit who gave the Word is present wherever it is preached and read. Our great Lawyer-Friend argues its truths with great persuasiveness and applies them to our lives. He helps us to think clearly about the things that count—the things that God has said to us through Jesus Christ.

Helping Us to Live Purely

The intellectual crisis—what to remember, how to understand—was not the only difficulty the disciples would encounter when Jesus took leave of them. There was a moral crisis as well. Their contact with him had put a difference between them and the rest of the world. His holiness and his love had spoiled them for their old ways of living.

New standards, new values, new motivations had been presented to them and demonstrated before their eyes. In Christ they saw a *quality of life* they had scarcely dreamed of. His compassion for the needs of men, his strength in the face of temptation, his courage before the mighty, his gentleness among the weak—all these put demands upon their lives for transformation. Jesus' example of love became their command to do the same.

And in Christ they felt a *consistency of life* that they could only wish for. What he purported to be was what he was. His inner life shielded no dark secrets. The inconsistency and hypocrisy that they saw around them and felt within them were absent in him.

Instead there was an aura of godliness—not a visible halo but a mood, an attitude, an atmosphere, a character of grace and glory that marked him off from all men. Yet this quality and this consistency he began to require from them.

Even when he was with them, setting his daily example and correcting their frequent mistakes, they still failed badly. Without him, how could they possibly fulfill his demands?

Here again, their help came from the Lawyer-Friend, the Spirit, sent to give them aid and comfort. Twice in our text Jesus called him the *Spirit of truth* (John 14:17; 15:26), and once he called him *the Holy Spirit* (John 14:26). Both of these terms speak of the way the Spirit helps us live purely. The *truth* which the Spirit brings is closely akin to his *holiness*.

Truth, in biblical teaching, is both thought and action. Christ not only *told* the truth; he *did* the truth. The Counselor whom he sent does not merely make us feel good; he leads us to do good. His holiness and his truth rub off on us. He reminds us of what Christ wants of us; he persuades us to imitate Christ; he empowers us to live a new kind of life. Not that we behave perfectly, but that our living has Christ's concerns and Christ's responses at its center.

One of my boyhood friends grew up to be a lawyer. His father, with an uncanny sense of humor, used to joke about this. "All my life," he claimed, "I have been getting in trouble. And all through those years I have been saying to myself, 'If only I had a son who was a lawyer to get me out of trouble.' But now my son is a lawyer. Does he get me out of trouble? No, he won't even let me get *into* trouble!"

That's the best kind of lawyer, one who heads off trouble before it starts. Often our great Lawyer-Friend does have to bail us out. What he really wants to do is to protect us from trouble before it begins by helping us to live purely.

Helping Us to Witness Boldly

In answer to the disciples' intellectual and moral crises Jesus asked the Father to send the Spirit. They also faced a crisis in *mission*. They were sent to preach the gospel to a world that rarely wanted to hear it: "Remember the word that I said to you, 'A servant is not greater than his master.' If they persecuted me, they will persecute you. . . . But when the Counselor [the *Paraclete*] comes, whom I shall send to you from the Father . . . he will bear witness to me;

and you also are witnesses, because you have been with me from the beginning" (John 15:20, 26–27).

Hatred and opposition were to run rampant. Christ's word not only blessed men, it judged them. The disciples were constantly tempted either to return to their old ways and forget their faith, or to huddle together in fear and protect their faith. Neither response was what Christ wanted. The world had to be reckoned with. God still loved it. His concern was just as great after Christ's crucifixion as it was before.

Bold, direct, powerful, forthright witness was what he wanted. And he sent the Spirit to witness to Jesus' lordship no matter how hostile and unbelieving the world was. The disciples were to be witnesses. They could not turn their backs on what they had seen and heard. The steady prodding of their Lawyer-Friend told them what to say and how to say it. And he does the same for us.

I am not a policeman, but I want to inform you of your rights. As a member of Jesus' family you have the right to be represented, strengthened, supported, encouraged by the greatest Lawyer of all. The chief Advocate of heaven and earth will take up your cause—the Holy Spirit of God, the Spirit of truth. You cannot get better help than that.

Prayer: Holy Father, if you are for me, who can be against me? Holy Spirit, if you are within why should I be troubled by anything outside me? Holy Savior, if you have promised to be with me to the end, why can't I make a new beginning? Father, Son, and Spirit, what I believe in my heart, do make come true in my life. Amen.

9. The Spirit
Helps Us Understand God's Wisdom

Yet among the mature we do impart wisdom, although it is not a wisdom of this age or of the rulers of this age, who are doomed to pass away. But we impart a secret and hidden wisdom of God, which God decreed before the ages for our glorification. None of the rulers of this age understood this; for if they had, they would not have crucified the Lord of glory. But, as it is written,

> *"What no eye has seen, nor ear heard,*
> *nor the heart of man conceived,*
> *what God has prepared for those who love him,"*

God has revealed to us through the Spirit. For the Spirit searches everything, even the depths of God. For what person knows a man's thoughts except the spirit of the man which is in him? So also no one comprehends the thoughts of God except the Spirit of God. Now we have received not the spirit of the world, but the Spirit which is from God, that we might understand the gifts bestowed on us by God. And we impart this in words not taught by human wisdom but taught by the Spirit, interpreting spiritual truths to those who possess the Spirit.

The unspiritual man does not receive the gifts of the Spirit of God, for they are folly to him, and he is not able to understand them because they are spiritually discerned. The spiritual man judges all things, but is himself to be judged by no one. "For who has known the mind of the Lord so as to instruct him?" But we have the mind of Christ (1 Cor. 2:6–16).

Wisdom is not easy to define. Questions flock to our minds at the very mention of the word. What is the relationship between wisdom and knowledge? How can we tell wisdom when we see it? Do we consider a person to be wise just because his opinions agree with ours? Can a person be intelligent and yet not be wise? Can a person have average intellectual capabilities and yet possess uncommon wisdom?

These are hard questions. They are made even harder when we realize that intelligence itself is difficult to measure. The famous IQ tests that we and our children have taken are under fire today. How accurate are they? Do they work equally well for children from various types of social, cultural, and economic backgrounds? Are the tests biased in favor of middle-class children who seem to score better on them than children from homes that are judged poorer in socio-economic terms? Even if the IQ tests are a fairly accurate gauge of a student's ability to do schoolwork, what do they tell about his chances of future success in life?

All of us know people whom we would classify as brilliant who lacked the discipline, the judgment, the motivation to do well after they left school. They drift from job to job or they finally land in some type of work that in no way taxes their potential. They just exist, frustrated that their talents are being squandered but seemingly unable to do anything about it.

And all of us know people who are not intellectually quick, yet seem to possess an uncommon amount of common sense. They do not have minds like calculators or memories like encyclopedias, but they do make sound decisions, give thoughtful advice, act sanely in all situations. We may not call them smart, but we do call them wise.

Wisdom and intelligence are not easy to define. And to judge the relationship between them we find difficult. Yet we know they are not the same thing. We find men and women who seem to have a lot of one and not much of the other. The person who understands and applies all he knows is rare indeed.

The Bible takes this problem of the nature of intelligence and wisdom one step further. It indicates that there are two types of wisdom—a wisdom that men have innately, and a gift that God gives specially. To his friends at Corinth Paul made this distinction: "And I was with you in weakness and in much fear and trembling; and my speech and my message were not in plausible words of wisdom, but in demonstration of the Spirit and power, that your faith might not rest in the wisdom of men but in the power of God.

"Yet among the mature," Paul went on to say, "we do impart wisdom, although it is not a wisdom of this age or of the rulers of this age, who are doomed to pass away. But we impart a secret and hidden wisdom of God, which God decreed before the ages for our glorification. None of the rulers of this age understood this; for if they had, they would not have crucified the Lord of glory" (1 Cor. 2:3–8).

Our problem has become more complex. We started out looking at the relationship of wisdom to intelligence, and decided that they were not the same: not all who are smart are wise. Now we have to push our conclusion ahead another notch: not all who are wise are *really* wise. There is, Paul has told us, a wisdom beyond our wisdom—an insight that comes from God, not dependent on human intellect or human wisdom: "But, as it is written,

> 'What no eye has seen, nor ear heard,
> nor the heart of man conceived,
> what God has prepared for those who love him,'

God has revealed to us through the Spirit" (1 Cor. 2:9–10). Three topics bob to the surface in this pool of ideas that Paul has put forth: first, why the Spirit can teach what no one else knows; second, what it is that the Spirit teaches; third, who the students are that the Spirit teaches.

Why the Spirit Can Teach

What no human teacher can figure out, the Holy Spirit knows. His is a wisdom that goes beyond anything the learned, the powerful, the wise men of our world can muster. Remember what Paul said earlier about the "rulers of this age." Smart men they were, skilled in the art of politics, learned in the disciplines of their day. Yet their wisdom led them astray just where they needed it most. They misunderstood the purposes of Christ; they misled the people who banked on their wisdom. They crucified "the Lord of glory." All the pooled insight of the Jewish and Roman leaders failed them in that moment. Their hour of truth found them filled with falsehood. Such are the ways of human wisdom when it tries to touch the things of God.

As Paul pondered this in his letter to the Romans he literally burst into song: "O the depth of the riches and wisdom and knowledge of God! How unsearchable are his judgments and how inscrutable his ways!

'For who has known the mind of the Lord,
    or who has been his counselor?'" (Rom. 11:33-34).

Paul answered his own question—"Who has known the mind of the Lord?"—in his words to the Corinthians. Certainly no ordinary human being, not even the wise and mighty rulers of our age. But God the Holy Spirit has known the mind of the Lord, "For the Spirit searches everything, even the depths of God" (1 Cor. 2:10). The word *searches* points to the Spirit's power to penetrate every issue in life, including the issues that God alone understands. He does not have to search to gain information; he knows everything. His searching is not for his benefit but for ours. His searching is like the probings of a giant searchlight that illuminates its findings for others to see.

The Spirit comprehends the thoughts of God. That's why he can teach. Paul's illustration is helpful. "For what person knows a man's thoughts except the spirit of the man which is in him? So also no one comprehends the thoughts of God except the Spirit of God" (1 Cor. 2:11). Even when we know people well, we cannot read their thoughts. We may be able to predict how they will respond to a certain situation, if we are well acquainted with them. But we can never be sure. In fact, we are likely to make them a little angry if we try to outguess them. Most people would rather speak for themselves than have outsiders guess their thoughts. The human spirit becomes readily outraged when someone tries to play God with its inner workings. With all of our insights into human behavior from literature, anthropology, history, sociology, psychology, and religion, the best way, the most reliable way, to find out what another person thinks is to have him tell you.

The human spirit—our self-consciousness, our inner awareness—must disclose itself to be understood. So it is in the realm of the divine. That's Paul's point. The Spirit of God, and he alone, can disclose the deep truths of God's will for human history. Without that revelation, human intellect and human wisdom can only make bad guesses.

The Spirit knows the plans of God. That's another reason why he can teach. "What God has prepared for those who love him, God has revealed to us through the Spirit" (1 Cor. 2:9–10). *Prepared* takes us back through that long—that eternal—process in which God laid and carried out his plan to bring salvation to our world. The Spirit was there all the time. He is the eternal Spirit. He knows, he shares in, the plans of God. We can count on him to help us understand. From beginning to end he is a participant in all that God is doing. One of his special tasks is to introduce us to these divine purposes, purposes which men and women who do not have God's Spirit can barely guess at.

What the Spirit Teaches

This leads us to say a word about the content of the Spirit's teaching. Just what is it that he helps us understand?

I should begin by saying what it is not. The Spirit of God does not ordinarily teach us mathematics or spelling. Our IQs do not go up when we become Christians. It is not academic learning that is the Spirit's curriculum.

Nor does he teach us technical things about the Bible or the Christian faith. The geography of the Holy Land, the meanings of Greek and Hebrew words, the dates and facts of church history are not what he teaches. We can study these on our own.

"A secret and hidden wisdom of God" is one way that Paul describes what the Spirit teaches (1 Cor. 2:7). Another way is this: "Now we have received not the spirit of the world, but the Spirit which is from God, that we might understand the gifts bestowed on us by God. And we impart this in words not taught by human wisdom but taught by the Spirit, interpreting spiritual truths to those who possess the Spirit" (1 Cor. 2:12–13). *Wisdom, gifts, spiritual truths*—this is the Spirit's curriculum.

The simplest way to put it is to call it the gospel in its *meaning* and *application*. What is God's wisdom? It is "Christ the power of God and the wisdom of God" (1 Cor. 1:24). What are God's gifts? They are the blessings of life and salvation given us in Christ, who himself is God's greatest gift to mankind. What are the spiritual truths? They are truths about Christ—who he is, what he does, what he demands—who is the Truth.

The Spirit does not convey academic or biblical knowledge. His work is not a substitute for scholarship. And he does not introduce us to vague ecstasies, new truths about other worlds, higher levels of inner consciousness, deeper interpretations of our dreams or other mystical experiences.

The Spirit of God is also the Spirit of Christ. He bears witness to Christ, God's Son and our Savior. And it is just here that we most desperately need his help. Academic learning we can get. There are colleges and universities within driving distance of almost all of us. There are encyclopedias and reference books on our shelves. Bible book stores teem with helps in understanding the geography, history, culture, language of biblical days. Mysticism we don't need. But if we did, there would be dozens of cults, both Eastern and Western, to introduce us to the psychic mysteries of life.

What we do need is to have our eyes and hearts opened to the wonder of God's ways as he has made them known in

Christ. This only the Spirit can do. But this he does well. It is the wisdom beyond wisdom. It is the wisdom that knows the limits of wisdom. He enlightens our minds to understand, and he bends our wills to obey.

He knows God because he is God. He knows us because he made us. He knows God's scheme to bring men and women to himself because he has played an eternal part in that scheme. No wonder he can teach.

Whom the Spirit Teaches

Even a child can understand the basic outlines of the Christian message—our need, God's love, our response of faith. But it is to the mature and the spiritual that the Spirit imparts these deeper insights (1 Cor. 2:6, 13). There are no first- or second-class citizens in God's kingdom. But like a family, there are younger and older children. There are Christians who are more developed, more mature, in their faith and in their understanding. To them the Spirit opens the deeper meanings of God's Word. He helps them apply the teachings of the Scriptures to every part of life. He helps them realize their areas of ignorance or disobedience and to do something about them.

Your intellectual ability is one thing. You may be blessed with brightness. Thank God. Your common sense is another thing. Use it well. But your spiritual wisdom is still another. It is *spiritual* wisdom because only God's Spirit can give it. But give it he does.

Prayer: Not to be smart as men measure smartness, not to be wise as men count wisdom do we ask, our Father. Grant us the maturity to have the wisdom beyond our wisdom, the wisdom of understanding and obeying your Word. Through Christ the living Word we pray. Amen.

10. The Spirit
Gives Gifts of Helpful Service

I appeal to you therefore, brethren, by the mercies of God, to present your bodies as a living sacrifice, holy and acceptable to God, which is your spiritual worship. Do not be conformed to this world but be transformed by the renewal of your mind, that you may prove what is the will of God, what is good and acceptable and perfect.

For by the grace given to me I bid every one among you not to think of himself more highly than he ought to think, but to think with sober judgment, each according to the measure of faith which God has assigned him. For as in one body we have many members, and all the members do not have the same function, so we, though many, are one body in Christ, and individually members one of another. Having gifts that differ according to the grace given to us, let us use them: if prophecy, in proportion to our faith; if service, in our serving; he who teaches, in his teaching; he who exhorts, in his exhortation; he who contributes, in liberality; he who gives aid, with zeal; he who does acts of mercy, with cheerfulness (*Rom. 12:1–8*).

A distinguished management consultant recalls a helpful story from his past. As a very young man he was an accomplished musician, a cellist with the Salzburg Symphony Orchestra in Austria. One afternoon he arrived at a special rehearsal and began to chat with the veteran cellist who played first chair in the orchestra. Like many musicians the senior cellist had strong feelings about orchestra conductors —they were overpaid and overpraised. They got the applause of the audience and the plaudits of the critics, while the players did the real work. These feelings bubbled to the surface as the young cellist conversed with the veteran.

"Who is conducting the orchestra today?" the younger man asked. "I don't know, and I don't care," sputtered the older musician. "Well, what music are we playing?" was the young man's next question. He and the senior cellist shared a music stand, and it was the duty of the young player to turn the pages of the score for them both. "What music are we playing?" the older man replied. "I don't know what music the rest of the orchestra are playing. But you and I are playing Beethoven's Fifth Symphony!"

We are relentlessly independent, if not obstinately contrary. We play our own scores in life regardless of who the conductor is or what the rest of the orchestra does. Frustrated soloists we often are, strumming our own tunes, hoping to be discovered by some *impressario* who will take us on the grand tour.

But this is not God's plan. He has called us to be servants, not soloists. He expects us to blend with the rest of the orchestra and to fix an eye on the baton with which he leads us.

Not everyone plays the same instrument. Not everyone has the same part. But all play together; and all have the same Leader. That's the way the Church is, or should be.

What makes the difference? What can change us from temperamental soloists committed to our independence even if it means disruption? What can make us willing, obedient servants of the divine Director?

Listen to Paul's words as he calls upon his friends at Rome to make just this kind of change: "I appeal to you therefore, brethren, by the mercies of God, to present your bodies as a living sacrifice, holy and acceptable to God, which is your spiritual worship. Do not be conformed to this world but be transformed by the renewal of your mind, that you may prove what is the will of God, what is good and acceptable and perfect" (Rom. 12:1–2).

Captured by the mercies of God, we begin to gear our lives for service even to the point of sacrifice. Indeed, sacrifice is no longer a cruel, harsh word to our ears. It is sacrifice—

Christ's sacrifice—that has saved us. It is his sacrifice that has brought freedom and dignity to our living. It is that sacrifice that displays God's mercy when we deserved his judgment. A happy, a healing word, *sacrifice* has become. His sacrifice asks for ours. The mercies of God demand our attention, our allegiance, our obedience.

Called from a conformity to the world, we begin to look to the will of God for direction in our lives. Human opinion, cultural standards, man-made customs have their influence on our lives to be sure. We don't live in a vacuum. My address is not a laboratory bell jar, a clinical sterilizer. I live in a home beside others, in a neighborhood to which many roads lead, roads which stretch out to a variety of races, customs, cultures. But calling me continually is the will of the God to whose mercies I have fallen captive. My address may look like my neighbor's, but the values, standards, priorities of my living must resemble God's.

Renewed in our thinking about our motives and purposes, we begin to give ourselves away in service. Our wrong thinking, Christ works to correct. Not what sounds good to us, but what is helpful to others, becomes the rule by which we choose our tunes. And all along the Spirit of God is with us and in us—reminding us of God's mercies, repeating to us God's call, revising our thoughts, and giving us gifts: gifts for helpful service.

Service Begins with Our Humility

None of God's work on our behalf is designed to make us proud. We may become proud, but our pride is not part of God's plan. In fact pride gets in the way of God's plan.

Pride may make us feel that we are too good to serve others. They ought to serve us. Or pride may lead to false conclusions about how fine our service is. We may serve a little, and then wait for the telegram to arrive informing us of the "Nobel Service Prize" that we have won for extraordinary work in the Kingdom. Work done in pride becomes a form of display. Work done merely for reward or recognition is bribery in another form.

Paul is frank, almost blunt, in his announcement that service begins with our humility: ". . . I bid every one among you not to think of himself more highly than he ought to think, but to think with sober judgment, each according to the measure of faith which God has assigned him" (Rom. 12:3). No room for mock humility here. That would not be sober judgment. And mock humility would also be an affront to the spiritual gifts—the measure of faith to trust God to work through us—that God has given each of us.

What we are, we are. What we have, we have. What we can do, we can do. We accept our abilities without building ourselves up or selling ourselves short. And whatever good gifts we have, God gets credit for. Service begins with our humility.

Service Builds on Our Unity

Pride has no place in our lives for another reason. We belong to each other. We are one body in Christ. Why should one member feel more important than another, when every member is part of every other member? What any member contributes, all other members share in. "For as in one body we have many members, and all the members do not have the same function, so we, though many, are one body in Christ, and individually members one of another" (Rom. 12:4–5).

No competition, no independence, no isolation within Christ's Body. We belong, we relate, we depend, we share. These are the verbs of our unity. Service builds on our unity. As we enjoy our oneness, as we draw strength from each other, as we take encouragement from our fellowship, we serve. Christ's Spirit, the source of our unity and our humility, is at work, drawing us to each other so that we will have the power to move out into the world. He begrudges—the Spirit does—all energy wasted on quarreling over differences or quibbling about distinctives. Christ has made us one. And that unity gives strength and freedom for service. We all do better, knowing that we do not do it alone.

Service Thrives on Our Diversity

God's Holy Spirit shows magnificent wisdom as he carries out his work. He uses every Christian as part of it. No member is left out. The Spirit is at work in Christ's Body, and every member has his task to do. No one is left out. That's one good thing. No one has to do too much. That's another. *Diversity* is the key word here. Christian service thrives on diversity.

"Having gifts that differ"—that's Paul's way of acknowledging our diversity. The one Spirit works differently in each life, giving to each believer the very gifts he wants him to have—the gifts of helpful service. Since the gifts we have do differ according to the way God's grace has given them, Paul draws a firm conclusion: "let us use them" (Rom. 12:6). The gifts are the Spirit's doing. We will be disobedient to him if we do not use his gifts for his purpose. And disobedience to the Holy Spirit is dangerous business.

Diversity there will be. God has so ordered it. Our lot is not to ask for other gifts or to try to exchange the ones we have, as though God's grace was a department store. Our lot is to rejoice in our diversity. Service thrives on it.

When we really believe that the one Holy Spirit has given a diversity of gifts to the Church, we will ask some key questions. What are my gifts? As a member of the Body of Christ, I can expect to have some gift or gifts. Christ's Spirit is in me, not only for my own good but for the good of the other members. What kind of service has he called me to do? What kind of special grace has he given me to do it well? I may not be able to answer these questions by myself. Other members of the body of Christ may have to help me. They may be able to spot my special function better than I. But I must believe that the Spirit has given me some gift that the rest of the Church can benefit from—and richly.

We also need to ask another question. What help do I need from my brothers and sisters in the Church? What gifts has God given them that I cannot do without? Our unity and our diversity are not theories to speculate about; they are practical Christian truths to be applied.

Not even the most gifted of us is spiritually self-supported. We have to have each other. Not even the least gifted of us is dispensible. Every member's contribution is a thing of joy and beauty to each other member.

A distinguished man of science, the president of a Canadian university, once told me that a whole university curriculum could be built around your little finger. Its complexity, its grace, its movements would lead you into many areas of learning. This is probably an exaggeration. But it does point out how useful and how fascinating every member of the human body is. The Christian Body, the Church, is no different.

Service Depends on the Spirit's Generosity

When we speak of the Spirit's gifts we are not talking about personal cleverness or innate ability. Nor do we mean natural talent in the normal sense of that word—a good ear for music, a retentive memory, graceful physical coordination. These are gifts of God, conveyed, I suppose, through our genes, part of our ancestors' legacy to us. And God cannot be excluded from the process.

But spiritual gifts are something else. They may build on our natural talent, but they go beyond it. They are the special skills that God has cultivated within us since we committed our lives to Christ and were baptized with that one Spirit.

Rhetoric may be a natural talent—the product of our heredity and environment. The "gift of gab" we may call it.

But the gift of *prophecy* is something else. It is a God-given inspiration that enables us to proclaim God's truth about Christ and what he means to us in power, clarity, and conviction. Apparently, the sovereign Spirit of God has chosen to give the gift of prophecy in varying measures to some members of the Body. Their responsibility is to use it in proportion to their faith, that is, to use it just as well as God enables them to (Rom. 12:6).

Service itself is called a gift. Though not so dramatic as prophecy, it is none the less important. Many Christians are needy. Their strength has failed them; their faculties are impaired; they may be cut off from their families. They need help. This help God has provided through the gift of service, the ability some Christians have to lend a helping hand to meet the physical, personal needs of others.

Teaching and *exhorting* are also listed as gifts. Here the emphasis is on understanding God's truth and urging others to obey it. These gifts would be used in the services and classes of the local congregations, where the Scriptures are studied and applied. You have all known people who had the gift of making the Bible clear, not only so that you understood it but so that you wanted to obey it. The Spirit does not leave so important an outcome to accident. He generously gives gifts to the members of the Church. Service depends on the Spirit's generosity.

Some of his gifts are so practical that we may not even consider them as gifts—*contributing* money or goods, *giving aid* to the helpless or needy, *showing mercy* to the oppressed or afflicted. Where these acts of care and concern go on, God's Spirit is at work—curbing our selfishness, overcoming our apathy, urging us to reach out to others. Such service is not natural. It is God-like, sparked by the Spirit's generosity.

Members of one body we are, players in God's great orchestra. We do not all play the same instruments at the same time. But we read from the same score, and we obey the same Conductor. Together we form a mighty symphony, a symphony of service. Service which God's Spirit alone has made possible with the gifts he has given so generously to his Church.

Prayer: Help us, Holy Father, to recognize our own gifts and those of others. Make us grateful to you for what we have as members of Christ's Body. Keep us playing your songs at your tempo, your songs of helpful service. In the name of Christ. Amen.

II. The Spirit
Gives Gifts to Equip the Church

I therefore, a prisoner for the Lord, beg you to lead a life worthy of the calling to which you have been called, with all lowliness and meekness, with patience, forbearing one another in love, eager to maintain the unity of the Spirit in the bond of peace. There is one body and one Spirit, just as you were called to the one hope that belongs to your call, one Lord, one faith, one baptism, one God and Father of us all, who is above all and through all and in all. But grace was given to each of us according to the measure of Christ's gift. Therefore it is said,

"When he ascended on high he led a host of captives,
and he gave gifts to men."

(In saying, "He ascended," what does it mean but that he had also descended into the lower parts of the earth? He who descended is he who also ascended far above all the heavens, that he might fill all things.) And his gifts were that some should be apostles, some prophets, some evangelists, some pastors and teachers, for the equipment of the saints, for the work of ministry, for building up the body of Christ, until we all attain to the unity of the faith and of the knowledge of the Son of God, to mature manhood, to the measure of the stature of the fulness of Christ; so that we may no longer be children, tossed to and fro and carried about with every wind of doctrine, by the cunning of men, by their craftiness in deceitful wiles (Eph. 4:1–14).

I was intrigued by the wording in the church bulletin. The order of service was rather formal, calling for a series of prayers in which the pastor and the congregation shared in turn. What intrigued me were the names assigned to the pastor and the congregation. The bulletin called the pastor 'the leader' and the congregation 'the ministers.' Leaders and ministers—they joined together in expressing praises and bearing requests to the Lord of the Church.

You can see why I was intrigued. When we think of the ministers of a church, we usually have in mind the pastoral staff—the senior minister and his assistants. We often distinguish between ministers and laymen, and we do so in a way that expresses rank. The Church is not a military platoon in which the pastor is the lieutenant and the members of the congregation are privates. It's not a naval ship where the pastors are the officers and the laymen are the able-bodied seamen. It is not a corporation where the pastors are the executives and the people are the secretarial and janitorial staff.

One of the reasons that our churches have had hard going is that we have misunderstood the nature of Christian ministry. We have forgotten that all God's people are ministers, that Christian ministry belongs to the whole Church.

It is the Holy Spirit that makes any Christian ministry possible. He supplies the power for ministry; he overcomes our shyness and helps us serve Christ boldly; he opens the hearts of those to whom we minister so that they will receive Christ's truth. Every believer has the Holy Spirit. Every believer has been made new by the Spirit's power. Every believer has been given the Spirit as a guarantee that God will complete his work of renewal and transformation. Every believer has been baptized by the Spirit so that he belongs to Christ and to every other believer. And every believer is called to minister in the power of the Spirit that has been given to him.

Not that every believer has the same ministry. We have already seen that the Church is like an orchestra, where each member plays his own instrument under the direction of Christ, who chooses the program and sets the tempo. We have also seen that the Church is like a body, where each member has its own function, yet all work together for the common good.

The Unity of the Spirit's Work

Unity and diversity are the twin themes whenever we hear about the Spirit's gifts. Life's strongest forces seem to be centrifugal. A church, a family, an organization is always in danger of flying apart. They are like the spinning disks at a carnival fun house. The speed at which they turn, the slipperiness of their hardwood finish, and the taper of their shape make it very difficult not to slide off.

Staying together takes a lot of energy and effort when the normal forces of life are working to separate us. No one ever had to work hard to build factions in a church; no one ever had to exert strenuous effort to form divisions, to spark competition, to separate member from member, to turn the members against the pastor. All of this comes easy. It is unity that takes work—not only ours but the Spirit's.

The Apostle Paul made this clear to his friends in the Ephesian letter as he issued *a call to unity*. "I therefore, a prisoner for the Lord, beg you to lead a life worthy of the calling to which you have been called, with all lowliness and meekness, with patience, forbearing one another in love, eager to maintain the unity of the Spirit in the bond of peace" (Eph. 4:1-3). Unity takes work. Lowliness, meekness, patience are not inborn virtues. They have to be cultivated. Yet without them unity is impossible. If one person is strong enough he can overpower another, crushing the individuality and squelching the spontaneity of that other human being. The stronger persons or group can then by sheer psychic energy impose their will on the opposition. The result may be cessation of conflict, an armistice. It is neither unity nor peace.

The Spirit who lives in every Christian is the one who calls us to unity and makes it possible for us to answer this call. He it is who helps us put down our fearfulness, our selfishness, our aggressiveness, in order that we may be tied together "in the bond of peace."

Paul not only issued a call to unity, but he outlined *the basis of our unity*. In one of the great summaries of Scripture he listed all the things we have in common, all the features of our faith that draw us together. "There is one body and one Spirit, just as you were called to the one hope that belongs to your call, one Lord, one faith, one baptism, one God and Father of us all, who is above all and through all and in all" (Eph. 4:4–6).

Like a net held together by cord after cord, the Church of Christ has a built-in unity that results from a number of undeniable factors. There is only one Holy Spirit. It would be blasphemy to deny this. To say that there is more than one Holy Spirit would be to confess polytheism—an unthinkable confession for men of the Bible who are relentlessly committed to monotheism, the belief in only one God. The one Holy Spirit who lives in every Christian knits the Church together into one Body. Because the Church is the Body of Christ she has only one Lord and one faith—that is, one body of doctrinal truths in which she believes. All believers are sons of the one Father, baptized by the one Spirit, and waiting for the one hope—the hope of being with and of being like Christ.

With this kind of basis for unity, all things that would separate Christians must be put aside as petty and trivial. Differences in outlook or perspective, in mood or attitude, in culture or custom, in talent or ability, in class or station, in race or sex, must all be put aside in the name of Christian unity—a unity which is the work of the Spirit of God himself.

The Diversity of the Spirit's Gifts

This spiritual unity is not uniformity. It does not insist that everyone do the same thing, act the same way, or minister in the same fashion. The Spirit of God does not transform persons into robots or rock them to sleep in boredom.

Instead, the Spirit brings to us the gifts which Christ wants us to have—and which his victory over sin and death has made possible. "But grace was given to each of us according to the measure of Christ's gift" (Eph. 4:7). This was Paul's way of saying that, through the Spirit, Christ has equipped each of us to play a special role in his program of ministry to the world. As the ascended Lord of heaven, he has the right to give whatever gifts he chooses to whomever he wishes. Like a conquering king he lavishes his spoils on those who share his victory. And as the Son of God who descended to earth and entered into the suffering circumstances of man, he knows what we need. He is no stranger to the apathy and hostility which are the setting for our ministry. He has been here. He knows what we need. Through the knowledge that comes from his humiliation, and the power that comes from his exaltation, Christ gives gifts to his people —gifts to equip the Church for her ministry.

Four gifts are mentioned specifically in this particular list: "And his gifts were that some should be apostles, some prophets, some evangelists, some pastors and teachers . . ." (Eph. 4:11). The Church, the Body of Christ, is one. Its leaders are several. Unity nurtured in diversity—this is the Spirit's pattern.

Apostles were the founders of the Church, the men whom Jesus selected as his special messengers. They had to be witnesses of the resurrection, people who had seen the risen Lord with their own eyes (1 Cor. 9:1). And they had to have received a special calling, to remember Christ's deeds and to understand his truths.

They were the sole links between Jesus and the later generations of his followers. Their calling was not based on their talent but on Christ's gift. Their success was assured not so much by their ability, as by the Spirit's power. They set the pace for the rest of the Church. They preserved and pro-

claimed the true faith. In the power of the Spirit they re-
called, wrote down, and made clear the words and deeds of
their Master.

We will not see their like again. They were there at the
beginning to do for the Church what needed to be done.
And they did it well. They were Christ's gift to the Church
to start it in the right direction. As his Spirit gave them
wisdom and power they wrote, spoke, and acted in Christ's
name.

Their authority was great. But they had no authority to
pass it on. Paul was an apostle. Timothy and Titus were not.
The apostles launched the ship on its course. No other crew-
men since have played such a crucial role.

Prophets also did their work at the beginning. Before the
Scriptures were completed, prophets were led by the Spirit
to expound the meaning of the Faith and to call people to
obedience and faith. Like their Old Testament counterparts,
the prophets of the Church were given special messages by
God—messages which might predict the future, but which
more usually proclaimed the Christian message in power and
authority. As the books of the New Testament were finished,
there was apparently less need for prophets. Their ministry
was taken over by the evangelists and the pastor-teachers,
whose gifts are mentioned next.

Evangelists were traveling preachers, whose special task
was to announce the good news of Christ's salvation. Missionaries, I suppose we might call them. Some persons within the
Church are especially called and equipped to make the
message clear to unbelievers and to encourage men and
women to answer Christ's call.

Pastors and teachers seem to be one office, an office that
ministers to people in the Church as evangelists seek to reach
those outside the Church. Personal help in times of need is
what the pastor or shepherd gives. His task is to keep the
flock from going astray, to feed it regularly, and to heal its
wounds. The two tasks, preaching and tending, go hand in

hand. Teaching is one of the ways a shepherd cares for his sheep. His teaching is kept realistic by his contacts with the people and their needs.

The Spirit was sent to make sure that Christ's Church carried out the Master's mission. One way he did this was to set up the various offices of leadership, offices based not on the people's choice but on the Master's gifts. The Church has survived and grown. Its mission has succeeded. Its scope is world-wide, and its message is well known. None of this is accidental. All of it is the Spirit's work. He gave the diversity of gifts that made it possible.

The Purpose of the Spirit's Gifts

The gifts are given for a purpose—not for the power of the leaders, but for the good of the Church: "for the equipment of the saints, for the work of ministry, for building up the body of Christ" (Eph. 4:12). Christians must be equipped to live, to grow, to work. The specially gifted leaders have this equipping of others as their aim. The work of ministry— all sorts of spiritual service from evangelism to social action —must go on. The leaders gifted by God's grace are supposed to enable the Church members to get on with this ministry. The Body of Christ is meant to be enlarged numerically and spiritually. It is the duty of leaders endued with divine gifts to encourage this growth.

The members of Christ's body are not spectators. They are players. They are called by Christ to add to their numbers and to strengthen each other in the faith. And they are to be coached and taught by leaders who are also players in the game. No one sits on the bench. All are on the field, committed to the contest, striving for victory. 'Leader' and 'ministers' that church bulletin said. That's the way the Church gets her work done.

". . . the unity of the faith . . . the knowledge of the Son of God . . . mature manhood . . . the measure of the stature of the fulness of Christ" (Ephesians 4:13)—these are our goals. We can have no higher ones. Thanks to the Spirit's gifts to the Church, they are not beyond our reach.

Prayer: Father, thank you for all your gifts—gifts of service, gifts of office, gifts of power. Teach us to discover them clearly and to use them well. For Jesus' sake. Amen.

12. The Spirit
Gives Gifts of Special Power

Now there are varieties of gifts, but the same Spirit; and there are varieties of service, but the same Lord; and there are varieties of working, but it is the same God who inspires them all in every one. To each is given the manifestation of the Spirit for the common good. To one is given through the Spirit the utterance of wisdom, and to another the utterance of knowledge according to the same Spirit, to another faith by the same Spirit, to another gifts of healing by the one Spirit, to another the working of miracles, to another prophecy, to another the ability to distinguish between spirits, to another various kinds of tongues, to another the interpretation of tongues. All these are inspired by one and the same Spirit, who apportions to each one individually as he wills (1 Cor. 12:4–11).

I suppose we can call it "the better mousetrap" syndrome. It has to do with competition, the drive to outdo each other. "Build a better mousetrap," the saying goes, "and the world will beat a path to your door."

Competition can be helpful and wholesome. The desire to excel can help a person or an organization to reach its full potential. Great art, fine music, deep learning, outstanding athletic achievement, startling inventions, distinguished political service are all, in part at least, the results of competition. Men and women have striven to do their best, improve their skills and abilities, to outdo others who are the outstanding practitioners in the same field.

But competition is also a risky business. It often takes us across the fine line where we not only help ourselves, but we hurt others; where we not only do well, but we do it at someone else's expense. When we win, someone else usually loses.

Sometimes we lose even when we win. We lose by becoming proud. We lose by taking credit for achievements that are really gifts. We lose by looking down on the so-called losers.

One of the great evidences of sin in our lives and in our society is the way in which competition frequently turns sour. Students today are keenly aware of the problem. They are asking for ways of grading and evaluating that will encourage them to do their best without some of the pressures that they feel in constant competition. Business executives, especially those in middle management, are looking for ways to replace competition for promotion and recognition with patterns of cooperation that will allow each person to perform well and to share in the rewards of success. The "better mousetrap" formula has its drawbacks as well as its benefits. Tension, fatigue, depression, discouragement, illness have been some of its less happy results. It may cause persons to cheat on their schoolwork or to falsify their progress reports in business.

A new approach is needed to our relationships with each other. We need to discover ways to make our best contribution to society, to the Church, to the Kingdom of God without being distracted by the negative results of competition.

It was this need for a new way that prompted the Apostle Paul to share some profound truths with his friends in Rome, Asia Minor (where Ephesus was), and Corinth. Churches in each of these places were becoming victims of the wrong kind of competition. The "better mousetrap" syndrome was taking its toll on them. Some members were elated with the special gifts they enjoyed and the power in the churches produced by those gifts. Others felt left out, inferior, useless. Paul sought to set both groups straight. Unity and diversity were the twin pins which Paul used to burst the balloon of false competition. Here's how he did this with the Corinthians, who were particularly inflated with the pride of spiritual accomplishment: "Now there are varieties of gifts, but the same Spirit; and there are varieties of service, but the same

Lord; and there are varieties of working, but it is the same God who inspires them all in every one. To each is given the manifestation of the Spirit for the common good" (1 Cor. 12:4–7).

Paul's statement is both clear and profound. The triune God—Father, Son, Spirit—is the source of our unity. Because all of us Christians worship the same God, because we all serve the same Lord, because we all have the same Spirit, we are all one. Whatever grouping we find ourselves in is less important than this basic unity. Furthermore, the gifts that we are given are not for our own profit but for the common benefit. No room for factiousness, pride, or competition here. God's Spirit is at work and he has shown us a new way.

The Gifts of Power

Paul went into detail as to what gifts he had in mind. This is the third set of spiritual gifts described in his letters. To the Romans he wrote of *gifts for helpful service*—gifts of prophecy, service, teaching, exhorting, contributing, giving aid, showing mercy. To the Ephesians he listed the *gifts that are used to strengthen the Church* for its ministry—gifts of leadership that enabled persons to serve as apostles, prophets, evangelists, pastors, and teachers. To the Corinthians he described *gifts of spiritual power:* "To one is given through the Spirit the utterance of wisdom, and to another the utterance of knowledge according to the same Spirit, to another faith by the same Spirit, to another gifts of healing by the one Spirit, to another the working of miracles, to another prophecy, to another the ability to distinguish between spirits, to another various kinds of tongues, to another the interpretation of tongues" (1 Cor. 12:8–10).

The utterance of wisdom is the first gift mentioned. We should certainly relate it to the spiritual wisdom that God has revealed in Jesus (1 Cor. 1:18–25). It is special insight into the meaning and application of the gospel. The person who has this gift will perform a valuable role in warning the Church if it is tempted to depart from sound doctrine or good behavior. This gift must have been particularly useful at a time when the New Testament writings were still incomplete, when the written words of Christ and the apostles were not yet widely circulated, and when few Christians were skilled in reading and writing.

The utterance of knowledge must be a gift quite like the utterance of wisdom. Paul seemed to connect it with understanding the mysteries of God. He said, for instance, "And if I have prophetic powers, and understand all mysteries and all knowledge . . . but have not love, I am nothing" (1 Cor. 13:2). God's ways are baffling; his mysteries are deep. The young churches stood in particular need of spiritual knowledge —knowledge of God's will and ways, knowledge of their response and mission. This knowledge the Spirit supplied through a special gift.

Faith as a gift of the Spirit is not the basic belief in God without which one cannot be a Christian. It is rather the gift to believe God for mighty works and wonders. Paul described it as "all faith, so as to remove mountains (1 Cor. 13:2)." It is that special faith which some people are given that enables them to do extraordinary acts for Christ. With this gift of faith whole tribes have been won to the Savior; enemies have been put down; prisons have become arenas for evangelism; entire towns have been rocked with the power of God.

Healing is mentioned specifically as a gift given to some members. Christ's ministry of healing was part of the way in which he announced the new age, the time of recovery and restoration, the time of salvation. The apostles had this power. They were the heralds, the spokesmen of the new age. Frequently they demonstrated God's dramatic power by healing the sick. From time to time, as it pleases God, he may grant gifts (Paul used the plural) to members of his Church to heal in Christ's name.

Working of miracles is mentioned along with healing.

Since healing has already been included among the gifts, we
are probably to assume that *miracles* refers to other acts of
power and wonder, like casting out demons. The New Testament is completely realistic. It knows that the context in
which we live is riddled with enemies of the human spirit—
death, disease, demonic opposition. Life is a contest, a war-
fare. The gifts of the Spirit are among the weapons which
God may furnish his Church to help it in times of dire
trouble.

Prophecy comes next in Paul's list. A gift central to the
ministry of the Church, it is the only one to be included in
all three lists—Romans, Ephesians, 1 Corinthians. Prophecy
may involve words about the future, but usually it is an inspired message to the present. It is the Spirit-powered procla-
mation of what Christ has done, what he will do, and what
he demands. As such it is a gift vital to the growth and health
of the Church.

The ability to distinguish between spirits is a gift that
some Christians have been supplied with, particularly in
settings where demon power is evident. In the early churches,
as in many contexts today, demons had to be faced. Imposters
were saying or doing outrageous things in the name of Christ.
They were encouraging heathen thoughts and activities
among Christ's people. They had to be exposed for what
they were. Their ecstatic speech, their claims to power, might
sound quite Christian. But the Holy Spirit saw to it that
among the believers were those who could tell the difference
between the work of God and the works of men or demons.

Various kinds of tongues remind us of what happened on
the day of Pentecost. Christians prayed with sounds and
words not of their own learning. And visitors from a host of
countries heard God's good news in their own language.
That unruly member, the tongue, with its great power to
bless and curse had been taken over by the Holy Spirit. The
experience at Pentecost was used to encourage the Christians
in their faith and to impress the non-Christians with God's
power. Countless thousands of Christians around the world

can testify that the same thing is happening to them today.

Interpretation of tongues is a gift that must be used side by side with speaking in tongues, whenever it takes place in a public meeting. It is not *experience* but *understanding* which is God's aim. The same Spirit who enables some people to speak in tongues enables others to share with the congregation the meaning of the unknown language so that all may understand.

The Need for Love

This is powerful talk, this discussion of spiritual gifts. The rich experience of being touched by God's Spirit was more than some Corinthians could take. They were victims of the "better mousetrap" syndrome. Things had happened to them spiritually that put them in the spotlight, that caused the world to beat a path to their door. Those who had powerful gifts grew arrogant; those who did not became frustrated. God's tremendous power was being used in ways that proved hurtful.

Paul's answer to this misuse of power was the proper application of love. In the very center of his teaching on spiritual gifts he inserted a poem of love (1 Cor. 13). "A still more excellent way" he called this (1 Cor. 12:31).

His point is simple. Power without love is noisy but empty, showy but purposeless, arresting but not satisfying. Power may be impressive at first glance, but it is love that lasts. "Make love your aim," Paul urged, "and earnestly desire the spiritual gifts, especially that you may prophesy" (1 Cor. 14:1). Here again Paul focused not on display of spiritual power, but on demonstration of the truth of Christ's gospel in inspired preaching and in loving actions.

The Call to Discipline

Paul could not close this lengthy section on spiritual gifts without calling the people to discipline in the use of the gift of tongues. This was apparently a major problem among the Corinthians, and has continued to be a problem in many places where the gift of tongues is exercised.

Paul laid down two basic rules. First, do not speak in tongues publicly unless someone is present to interpret. Second, let there be only two or three messages in tongues in any public service (1 Cor. 14:27–28).

Though tongues and interpretation are spiritual gifts, a person must control their use, according to Paul. They must be used publicly not to distract, but to build up the Church. Otherwise, they should be used only in private—to encourage the spiritual growth of the believer who prays in another tongue.

The Spirit's work is heady like new wine. We are not to close our hearts to it, but we are to exercise any gifts we may have under the discipline of the Scriptures. The Spirit who gives the gifts and the Spirit who inspired the Word are one. There will be no conflict between gifts properly used and the Scriptures correctly read.

The Spirit's greatest work is to bind God's people together in love. If the "better mousetrap" syndrome attacks us and unchristian competition and divisiveness set in, the gifts must take second place to the law of love. The Spirit who gives the gifts is the Spirit of love. Nothing less than love among all the members of Christ's body is his aim. Ours must be the same.

Prayer: Lord of the Church, give to us—your members—the gifts we need and the grace to use them wisely. In Jesus' name. Amen.

13. The Spirit Grows His Special Fruit

For you were called to freedom, brethren; only do not use your freedom as an opportunity for the flesh, but through love be servants of one another. For the whole law is fulfilled in one word, "You shall love your neighbor as yourself." But if you bite and devour one another take heed that you are not consumed by one another.

But I say, walk by the Spirit, and do not gratify the desires of the flesh. For the desires of the flesh are against the Spirit, and the desires of the Spirit are against the flesh; for these are opposed to each other, to prevent you from doing what you would. But if you are led by the Spirit you are not under the law. Now the works of the flesh are plain: immorality, impurity, licentiousness, idolatry, sorcery, enmity, strife, jealousy, anger, selfishness, dissension, party spirit, envy, drunkenness, carousing, and the like. I warn you, as I warned you before, that those who do such things shall not inherit the kingdom of God. But the fruit of the Spirit is love, joy, peace, patience, kindness, goodness, faithfulness, gentleness, self-control; against such there is no law. And those who belong to Christ Jesus have crucified the flesh with its passions and desires.

If we live by the Spirit, let us also walk by the Spirit. Let us have no self-conceit, no provoking of one another, no envy of one another (Gal. 5:13–26).

Do you have a favorite portrait of Jesus? A picture that captures for you the remarkable characteristics of the One whom we call Lord and Savior? Has any artist that you know been able to catch with brush and oils Christ's unique combination of majesty and humility, of strength and gentleness, of power and love?

Many have tried, and some have been able to do better than others. There's the portrait of Christ in Gethsemane, kneeling against a rock, wrestling with the will of God amidst the shadows of the garden, while his disciples huddle in the background, escaping into sleep. Or there's the contemporary picture that shows Jesus surrounded by children clothed in modern dress. A little girl sits on Jesus' knee, holding his open palm in one hand while pointing to it with her other. The inscription under the painting seems to overhear the question the children are putting to the Savior in their naive, straightforward way: "What happened to your hand?"

In some of your homes there hangs the picture of Christ at the door. It is an illustration of the familiar words of Revelation 3:20—"Behold, I stand at the door and knock; if any one hears my voice and opens the door, I will come in to him and eat with him, and he with me." You know the picture. Jesus has a lamp in his hand. The door, slightly overgrown with vines and shrubbery, has no visible handle. It can be opened only from the inside. The patience and the persistence of Jesus are what the artist has grasped in this painting.

Other paintings focus on other aspects of Jesus' character. Sallman's head of Christ is familiar to many of you. Gentle and kind the Savior appears in that portrait, almost too sweet, too feminine for the tastes of some. In contrast, there is a contemporary picture that tries to catch the ruggedness of Christ. A sturdy mallet is clutched in the massive fist of a carpenter. There is firmness and resolve in his face. "I will get the job done," his eyes seem to say. "Make no mistake about that."

From Michelangelo, with his delicate Pietà—a statue of the broken body of Jesus held in Mary's arms—to Dali, with his surrealistic painting of the crucifixion which combines suffering and lordliness, sculptors and artists have imagined for us what Jesus looked like. They have done this so persistently and so effectively that we think we know what he looks like. We recognize his picture no matter who has painted it.

We may be able to judge who the better artists are, but we cannot tell who has captured the best likeness of Christ. Art is one thing; accuracy is another. The fact is, we do not know what Jesus looked like. We know much of what he said. We have accounts of many of his deeds. But the New Testament authors give us no picture of his face or frame. Was he short or tall? We don't know. Were his eyes blue, black, brown? We have no idea. How long was his hair? What shape was his face? Did he wear a beard? We can only guess.

The words, the deeds, the character of Jesus—these the gospels and the epistles make clear. Portraits there are, and many, in the New Testament. But they focus on the inner life of Jesus and on his unique mission, not on his looks.

One such portrait—one of the finest, in fact—was painted by Paul in Galatians, where he listed the fruit of the Holy Spirit. "But the fruit of the Spirit is love, joy, peace, patience, kindness, goodness, faithfulness, gentleness, self-control; against such there is no law" (Gal. 5:22–23). It takes no great insight to see that Paul was summing up the personal qualities of Jesus Christ, who himself sat for this portrait. What *does* take insight is to see how these magnificent attributes can ever develop in us. That's where the Spirit's work comes in.

Growth Takes Place in a Context of Conflict

His work is badly needed. For one thing, we live in a context of conflict. Growth, if it is to take place at all, takes place in a setting of opposition. Jesus warned his followers of this. He spoke of Satan's opposition that would produce tribulation in the world (John 16:1–11, 33). He spoke also of the hatred with which the people of the world would treat Christians (John 15:18–25). Christian growth goes on in an atmosphere of hostility. Jesus made this clear. But he also made it clear that this hostility could not choke off the Spirit's life-giving waters. Growth would take place despite the opposition. God the Holy Spirit could outdo any enemy.

Paul picked up this theme of *growth in the midst of conflict* in his letter to the Galatians. But here, the battle is waged not with the world or the devil but with the flesh. "But I say, walk by the Spirit, and do not gratify the desires of the flesh. For the desires of the flesh are against the Spirit, and the desires of the Spirit are against the flesh; for these are opposed to each other, to prevent you from doing what you would" (Gal. 5:16–17). Human lust, human ambition, human rebellion, human selfishness—these are what Paul means by *flesh*. It is that built-in drive to protect ourselves and hurt others, to worship things and ignore God, to call good things bad and bad things good.

The Spirit's work of restoration has to reckon with God's great enemy—Satan. And it has to take place in the midst of the world, where men and women look at life from every point of view except God's. Furthermore, it has to reckon with the deep drives to think wrong thoughts and to perform wrong acts that lie within each of us.

In other words, the Spirit's work of growth does not take place in a well-cleared field, but in a weed patch. The Holy Spirit is like a relief pitcher that comes out of the bull pen and has to throw strikes against the top hitters in baseball in the midst of a partisan crowd that boos his every move.

The flesh—our flesh—is a formidable enemy. Paul uses the term *flesh* for good reasons. The enemies of the faith in Galatia were putting a lot of emphasis on it. *Circumcision*— a minor operation which leaves a mark on human flesh—was taught to be the badge of true discipleship. Gentile men were being called to become Jews in order to be Christians. The *law* of Moses was extolled as the way to discipline human urges. This too made people conscious of the flesh. Over-attention to the flesh aggravated rather than alleviated the problem. Preoccupation with human flesh gave the flesh room to do its awful work. Thinking about an itch in-

creases the desire to scratch, and scratching further irritates
the itch. So it is with the flesh. Another answer is needed.

Ignore the flesh, and its evil deeds will break out on your
blind side. Cater to the flesh, and it will repay your kindness with the back of its hand. Its works are just plain evil.

These works—our sinful drives—attack the human body
in the forms of "immorality, impurity, licentiousness." They
lead us away from true worship into "idolatry" and "sorcery." They turn men into beasts who fight each other in
"enmity, strife, jealousy, anger, selfishness, dissension, party
spirit, envy." They aim to destroy human personality through
the ravages of "drunkenness, carousing, and the like." No
wonder Paul concluded this awful list of the works of the
flesh with a warning "that those who do such things shall not
inherit the kingdom of God" (Gal. 5:19–21).

Growth Results in a Change of Character

Happily, Paul did not stop with a warning. He brought
the encouraging news that God's Spirit is stronger than
human flesh. Flesh and Spirit war against each other. They
have to. Left on its own the flesh produces terrible results.
When the Spirit intervenes, new things happen. Life changes;
character is refined; fruit begins to grow.

Fruit in Scripture is often used to describe traits of character which are worth cultivating. The prophet Isaiah likened
Israel to a vineyard in which God wanted to grow fine
grapes. Instead, at harvest time all he found were wild grapes,
small and sour. The fine grapes that he looked for were
justice and righteousness. The wild grapes that grew instead
were bloodshed and a cry of oppression (Isa. 5:1–7).

Similarly in John 15, Jesus urged his disciples to bear fruit
by abiding in him. He is the vine; we are the branches. The
fruit he asks for is love: "This is my commandment, that you
love one another as I have loved you" (John 15:12).

It comes as no surprise, then, that Paul spoke of the finest
personal qualities as *fruit*. Charles E. Fuller had been raised

on his father's orange ranch in Redlands, California. As an adult he himself had grown oranges and managed packing houses where oranges were prepared for shipping. He knew a lot about fruit.

One day Dr. Fuller and I were talking about the fruit of the Spirit, and especially the first fruit mentioned by Paul— love. Dr. Fuller said, "You know, Dave, the fruit of the Spirit is like a Valencia orange. Hold it in your hand and you have one orange. Peel it and break it open and you have eight segments—one orange and eight parts. *Love* is the fruit of the Spirit. And love has eight facets that are mentioned by Paul: joy, peace, patience, kindness, goodness, faithfulness, gentleness, self-control.

Love, joy, and peace are our *responses to God's grace* in our lives. As the Holy Spirit helps us to appreciate the forgiveness that Christ has provided, basic changes take place within us. We reach out to treat others with concern and dignity—that's *love*. We develop a deep-seated conviction that God will make everything in life turn out all right— that's *joy*. We relax in our new relationship with God, knowing that God is for us and that he is greater than anyone who is against us—that's *peace*.

Patience, kindness, and goodness describe *our responses to the needs of others*. As the Holy Spirit leads us on to Christian maturity, we can not only put up with harsh treatment without getting hostile, but we can also reach out to do positive good without becoming proud. *Patience* means long-suffering, the ability to endure difficult circumstances without losing our tempers. *Kindness* speaks of a positive disposition toward others, especially those who need our help. *Goodness* goes a step beyond disposition or attitude to action in loving, righteous deeds toward people in need.

Faithfulness, gentleness, self-control refer to *our inner attitudes of discipline*. As the Holy Spirit nurtures our personal growth, we find ourselves becoming more stable in conduct. *Faithfulness* means reliability as we keep our word, follow through on our commitments, make ourselves consistently available to those who count on us. *Gentleness* means that we do all of this graciously, not feistily or aggressively. It means that we are at peace with our power so that we don't use it arrogantly or hurtfully. *Self-control* describes the discipline of our appetites, urges, and inclinations. It speaks of moderation and balance, of good taste and good judgment in our habits, our words, our actions.

These are the fruit of the Spirit, the ways in which love regulates our conduct and shapes our character. When the Spirit does his work, the flesh is kept in hand and the law is not needed. Hardly anything the Spirit does is greater evidence of his power than his ability to replace the works of the flesh, vile as they are, with the fruit of the Spirit, vital as it is. This is God's doing, wonderful in our eyes. *This growth takes outside help.* That's a point that should not be missed. Artificial fruit may look all right on the table, but it contains neither flavor nor nourishment. Our attempts to produce the Spirit's fruit by self-improvement programs are just as flat and useless.

These descriptions of what the Spirit can do in us sometimes discourage me. There's a gap between what God promises to do and what I find happening in my own life. I need to remember that *this growth takes time.* Walking in the Spirit is done only a step at a time. Growth inches its way to maturity. Take the long view. See how far you have come in the past few years. Rejoice in the growth you have gained. And then trust the Spirit to keep on working. Don't keep pinching the fruit to see how ripe it is. Let it grow at its own pace.

What is really encouraging about our growth under the Spirit's cultivation is that *this growth makes us like Christ.* It is his portrait that Paul painted, one of the great portraits in that gallery of spiritual art—the Bible. As we grow, we grow into his likeness. No wonder we get impatient. We want to be like him. No wonder we can *be* patient. Being like him is worth waiting for and working at. With the Spirit's help we do both.

Prayer: Heavenly Father, we are hungry for your fruit. We have tasted of Christ's goodness and we want to be more like him. You have promised that those who hunger and thirst after righteousness will be filled. Do that for us, in Jesus' name. Amen.

14. The Spirit Fills Us
with Power to Worship and Serve

Look carefully then how you walk, not as unwise men but as wise, making the most of the time, because the days are evil. Therefore do not be foolish, but understand what the will of the Lord is. And do not get drunk with wine, for that is debauchery; but be filled with the Spirit, addressing one another in psalms and hymns and spiritual songs, singing and making melody to the Lord with all your heart, always and for everything giving thanks in the name of our Lord Jesus Christ to God the Father (Eph. 5:15–20).

A friend and I were talking about the humdrum nature of a lot of the work we do. Parts of it are exciting, yet much of it is routine. As we reflected on this, I remarked on how easy it is for outsiders to misunderstand the nature of my job. To those who don't know, a seminary president's ministry may look like nothing but excitement. Contact with bright students, friendships with learned professors, access to church leaders, opportunity for travel—these experiences *do* have a measure of excitement to them. But much of what I do has a lot of sameness and even dullness to it. Talk on the phone with critics as well as friends, glance through a stack of mail and try to pick out the most urgent, chat with members of our administrative team about problems of budgets or buildings, recommend a book to a student who is stuck on a problem in his research—so goes the day.

As my friend said, when we talked about this, "Most jobs —even the best ones—have only a few high moments. The rest of the time is spent just washing the dishes!" A few months later I saw the seminary painter chipping away at old paint for several hours straight. I said to him, "Lem, you may not realize it, but much of what I do is like chipping paint." This is not to say that I would want his job or that he would want mine. To each his own. God has given Lem gifts to paint well, and he has equipped and called me to do what I have to do.

My point is simply this. Much of life, even for those of us who seem to be surrounded by excitement, is tedious at best. One day blends into another as the endless routine runs its course.

Thrill-seeking types of people find life hard to take. They flit from job to job, relationship to relationship, pleasure to pleasure, looking for something to lift life above its tedium.

When we add pain and pressure to the tedium of life the situation proves even more vexing. Lots of people walk through life with lumps of anxiety in their stomachs as big as turnips. Or they grope their way along with chests so tight they feel as though someone had planted his boot on their bosom.

Far too many thrill-seeking and pressure-driven people are taking refuge in alcohol. Its narcotic seems to ease the anxiety and lift the pressure. The turnip in the tummy is reduced to the size of a golf ball, and the boot pressing the chest feels more like a leather glove after three or four stiff drinks. Something like one person in every twenty in the United States has chosen to deal with life's problems in this way.

There is nothing new about this solution. Some of the earliest stories in the Bible point out the dangers of escape into alcohol. In virtually every society, in every era of history, on every continent, men and women have tried to short-circuit the tedium and pressure of life by intemperate drinking. Corn, barley, sweet potatoes, wheat, rye, sugar cane, rice, grapes, fruits and berries all yield alcohol when properly fermented and distilled. Man's ingenuity and nature's bounty have combined to give people almost everywhere access to alcohol in sufficient measure to give them relief and trouble.

Man in his sinfulness has abused God's bounty and produced an antidote to his problems that has proved costly. The cure has done more damage than the disease. In fact the cure has become another, more destructive, disease. But God's grace has not abandoned man either to his tedium and pressure or to his drunken solution.

Where sin abounds, grace abounds all the more. In his grace God has given us his Holy Spirit to lead us out of our despair—including our despair over life's monotony and pain. Not wine, but the Holy Spirit is God's answer to our needs. "And do not get drunk with wine, for that is debauchery; but be filled with the Spirit" (Eph. 5:18).

Paul's advice is well founded. He had seen enough of drunkenness in his travels to the great pagan cities of the Mediterranean to know the futility of that solution to our human needs. And he had seen enough of the Spirit's power in his own life and the lives of his Christian friends to know that God's answer was more than adequate. Two special aspects of this answer stood out as he wrote his friends in Ephesus about the Spirit's help. The Spirit helps us live wisely, and the Spirit helps us worship joyfully. Wisdom and joy are a hard combination to beat, when it comes to digging meaning out of life's perplexities. Life can be more than washing dishes while we wait for a few high moments, if the Holy Spirit is at work within us.

The Spirit Helps Us Live Wisely

The *filling* of the Spirit is a subject that takes some studying. Frequently, the Bible uses an expression like "filled with the Spirit" to describe the special power or ability that God gave for special tasks. For instance, of Bezalel, the man whom God chose to design and build the Tabernacle in the wilderness, we read: "and I have filled him with the Spirit of God, with ability and intelligence, with knowledge and all craftsmanship, to devise artistic designs, to work in gold, silver, and bronze, in cutting stones for setting, and in carving wood, for work in every craft" (Exod. 31:3–5). A master artisan is filled with God's Spirit to make his work beautiful and accurate.

Similarly, the filling of the Spirit has often enabled men or women in the Bible to speak with a knowledge, accuracy, and power beyond their natural resources. John the Baptist was filled with the Spirit from his mother's womb to prepare him for his ministry of turning many of the sons of Israel to the Lord their God (Luke 1:15). His mother, Elizabeth, was filled with the Holy Spirit as she spoke her words of blessing to Mary, the mother of our Lord (Luke 1:41). John's father, Zechariah, was filled with the Holy Spirit to announce the meaning of John's mission (Luke 1:67). In much the same way Peter and Paul were filled with the Spirit to declare the faith in the face of great opposition (Acts 4:8; 13:9).

What Paul wrote about to the Ephesians is a somewhat different aspect of the Spirit's work. There he did not have in mind inspiration for a special occasion, a powerful filling for a definite assignment. Rather, he was speaking of our constant walk with God. He was pointing to the way we conduct ourselves in the secular contexts where we live. How do we live in purity and power in settings that conspire to defile and debilitate us?

The Spirit's help in these circumstances is indispensable. Not on an occasional basis, but permanently. The Church of Christ that began at Pentecost with the Spirit's filling needs to continue the same way. The fact that the Spirit does help us to live wisely is one point Paul makes. These are his words: "Look carefully then how you walk, not as unwise men but as wise, making the most of the time, because the days are evil" (Eph. 5:15–16).

Wisdom in the use of time—this is one of the Spirit's gifts to us. Time that seems so tedious, time that winds us up with tension, time that, by spurts, hangs heavy and runs short can be bought up and filled with opportunity when God gives us wisdom. One of the things that Jesus Christ has done is to turn periods of time into moments of opportunity. When he lived on earth Jesus often spoke of his "hour," not so much as a fixed period of time, but as the magnificent opportunity when God would show his glory to men and women through the triumphant death of his Son. "The acceptable year of the Lord" (Luke 4:19) is not just the record of the earth's journey around the sun; it is that fertile period of ministry that has now lasted centuries— the period when people everywhere may put their trust in Jesus Christ and avoid the wrath to come.

Moments, hours, days, years become rich with meaning when we see them as opportunities to make God's love known. Evil days these are, and they demand wisdom to do our best in the midst of them. They are evil because they are largely in the control of evil men. Christians are *not* the ones who usually set the pattern and style of our living. Secular persons, innocent of or hostile to any knowledge of God, commonly do. Because the days are evil, the time to bring remedy is short. Conversion or judgment are the two options that God normally offers the sons of men. The Holy Spirit wants to fill us with wisdom so that we can not only avoid the corruptions of the world but make some inroads for change.

To do this we also need *wisdom to understand God's will.* "Therefore do not be foolish, but understand what the will of the Lord is" (Eph. 5:17). "What the will of the Lord is" —that is life's central question. Pressures from inside and outside of us are trying to regulate our priorities, govern our use of time and energy, determine our values, mold our purposes. But what really counts is knowing God's will and understanding how to carry it out. For this we have the Spirit's help. The Lord of the Church taught his followers to pray "thy will be done on earth as it is in heaven." And that same Lord has sent his Spirit to help us fulfill that command. To the extent that we are filled with the Spirit, to that extent we will understand and do God's will, making the most of every opportunity.

The Spirit Helps Us Worship Joyfully

Tedium and pressure there may be. Life does have a lot of dishwashing and paint chipping to it. But the Holy Spirit, as he fills our lives, can do a lot more for us than wine, even of the finest vintage. He helps us live wisely, and he helps us worship joyfully. The Christians in those early days really enjoyed getting together. The reports of their meetings make us envious, until we remember that we, today, worship the same risen Lord as they did. We have access to the same Spirit, who lives within us and wants to fill us. Listen again to what happens to our worship when the Spirit fills his people; hear how it comes alive: "And do not get drunk with wine, for that is debauchery; but be filled with the Spirit, addressing one another in psalms and hymns and spiritual songs, singing and making melody to the Lord with all your heart, always and for everything giving thanks in the name of our Lord Jesus Christ to God the Father" (Eph. 5:18–20).

As the Spirit has more and more control of our lives we are able to *encourage each other in the faith*. Hymns, songs, psalms, snatches of Scripture come to mind that will comfort and strengthen the other members. Many churches, by the way, are recovering the sense of joy and spontaneity which an informal hymn-sing provides. The Spirit of God uses music in an amazing way to speak to the spirits of men.

And the Spirit, filling our lives with his presence, helps us to *praise God wholeheartedly*. The Spirit is a liberator, though an orderly one. He is not the author of confusion, freeing us to do and say whatever we like whenever we like. He is the Lord of liberty and of order. He sets us free to praise God, to celebrate his deeds, to adore his name. Free from the distractions of our own needs, free from the tensions of our society, free from the tedium and pressure of life itself, we focus on the greatness and goodness of God—the God who can meet our needs, support us in the tensions, raise us above the tedium, steady us amid the pressures.

And the Spirit, flooding our experience with God's own peace and joy, can help us to *give thanks always and for everything in Christ's name*. We can even give thanks for what seem to be monotonous or painful circumstances. God's love is sure. God's will is good. God's purposes will win. The Spirit-filled person knows this and gives thanks.

Drunkenness brings temporary relief; the Spirit's presence is permanent. Drunkenness dulls our judgment, keeps us from thinking straightly, seeing clearly, reacting wisely; the Spirit's insight is unfailing, penetrating even the deep thoughts of God. Drunkenness is destructive, leading to greater dependence and decadence; the Spirit's mission is positive, renewing us stage by stage in Christ's likeness. Drunkenness brings social devastation, splitting families, jeopardizing business, threatening whole communities; the Spirit's filling helps to heal, pointing men and women to the one true God who alone can save.

Life has its humdrum sides, and we are all tempted to seek relief for our thirst for meaning and excitement. Let it be to God's Spirit that we turn. He who drinks to the full of *him* knows satisfaction at its best.

Prayer: Our heavenly Father, save us from the foolishness that drives us to drink the wrong things in the wrong places. Let the new wine of your Spirit liven and brighten our days in wise living and joyful worship. In Jesus' name. Amen.

15. The Spirit Brings the New Age

*Are we beginning to commend ourselves again? Or do we
need, as some do, letters of recommendation to you, or from
you? You yourselves are our letter of recommendation,
written on your hearts, to be known and read by all men;
and you show that you are a letter from Christ delivered by
us, written not with ink but with the Spirit of the living
God, not on tablets of stone but on tablets of human hearts.*

*Such is the confidence that we have through Christ toward
God. Not that we are sufficient of ourselves to claim anything
as coming from us; our sufficiency is from God, who has
qualified us to be ministers of a new covenant, not in a
written code but in the Spirit; for the written code kills, but
the Spirit gives life.*

*Now if the dispensation of death, carved in letters on stone,
came with such splendor that the Israelites could not look at
Moses' face because of its brightness, fading as this was, will
not the dispensation of the Spirit be attended with greater
splendor? For if there was splendor in the dispensation of
condemnation, the dispensation of righteousness must far
exceed it in splendor. Indeed, in this case, what once had
splendor has come to have no splendor at all, because of the
splendor that surpasses it. For if what faded away came with
splendor, what is permanent must have much more splendor.*

*Since we have such a hope, we are very bold, not like
Moses, who put a veil over his face so that the Israelites might
not see the end of the fading splendor. But their minds were
hardened; for to this day, when they read the old covenant,
that same veil remains unlifted, because only through Christ
is it taken away. Yes, to this day whenever Moses is read a
veil lies over their minds; but when a man turns to the Lord
the veil is removed. Now the Lord is the Spirit, and where*

the Spirit of the Lord is, there is freedom. And we all, with unveiled face, beholding the glory of the Lord, are being changed into his likeness from one degree of glory to another; for this comes from the Lord who is the Spirit (2 Cor. 3:1–18).

It happens every Christmas and almost any birthday. We have a hard time understanding it, even though we have seen it frequently. A young child is given a beautifully wrapped package. Eagerly he tears it open, and eagerly we watch his excitement grow. With clutching hands and wide eyes he takes the object out of the box—the latest mechanical toy— and gasps his thanks.

His older sister's turn comes next. Her package, big as she is, contains a doll that walks and talks. She squeals with glee, and gives the huge doll a wobbly hug.

The adults have noted the youngsters' responses with great satisfaction. The time spent in finding the gifts has been worth it. The effort expended in wrapping and hiding them has paid off. The outlandish price of the toys seems justifiable in light of the joy they will provide.

Then it happens. The grownups turn their attention to other matters—their own gifts, the holiday meal, conversation with each other, football on television. During a lull in the festivities they decide to check on Tommy and Susie, to behold the sheer delight with which they revel in their new toys. But what do they find? The mechanical contraption sits idle in the corner. The walking doll lies prone behind the couch. What about the children? Well, Tommy has built a fort out of the box that Susie's doll came in, and Susie has made a party costume from the wrappings and ribbons that held Tommy's toy.

In the strange value system of childhood, the containers have been deemed more important than the contents. The wrappings have outshone the gifts.

From the beginning, the people of Christ have shown their childishness by making that same mistake. More than once, the apostles—particularly Paul, who was especially sensitive to the problem—had to warn the early Christians not to yield to this temptation.

The precise form of the temptation varied from situation to situation. But usually it went something like this. False teachers would follow in the tracks of an apostle and try to take advantage of the simple faith of the new converts. These impostors would often claim special authority from apostles or churches. At times they even carried letters of recommendation to establish their credibility (2 Cor. 3:1). Then they usually added something to the apostles' teaching—legalistic regulations about diet, dress, rituals, holy days, and circumcision. These tangible requirements were often attractive to the young believers. They felt as though they were doing these for God—disciplining themselves, regulating their lives, making sacrifices. They were demonstrating how seriously they took their commitment to Christ.

Paul's response was always direct and uncompromising. "Don't trade the gift for the wrappings! Don't confuse the contents with the container!" God used the law, with its detailed regulations for all of life, as part of his preparation for the gospel—that was Paul's point. Now that Christ had come he had brought a new age, a fresh way of working. Not the law governing life from without, but the Spirit changing life from within—that was God's new way.

The false teachers were deceivers who themselves were deceived. Paul and the other true apostles were "ministers of a new covenant, not in a written code but in the Spirit; for the written code kills, but the Spirit gives life" (2 Cor. 3:6).

To make the issues plain, Paul used the sharpest possible contrast between the law that the false teachers were trying to impose and the new way that Paul proclaimed: "Now if the dispensation of death, carved in letters on stone, came with such splendor that the Israelites could not look at Moses' face because of its brightness, fading as this was, will not the dispensation of the Spirit be attended with greater splendor?" (2 Cor. 3:7-8).

There was much that was splendid about the old age, the Old Testament period. After all, God was at work. It was he who gave the law, who revealed himself to Moses, who guided the destiny of Israel. The scene on Sinai shone with splendor. God spoke and Moses listened, his face aglow from his encounter with the glory of God: "The glory of the Lord settled on Mount Sinai, and the cloud covered it six days; and on the seventh day he called to Moses out of the midst of the cloud. Now the appearance of the glory of the Lord was like a devouring fire on top of the mountain in the sight of the people of Israel" (Exod. 24:16-17).

Bright as that old picture was, God's new way is even more splendid: "Will not the dispensation of the Spirit be attended with greater splendor?" *The dispensation of the Spirit*—this was Paul's name for the new age that Christ had brought to human history, the most splendid age that man has yet seen.

The dispensation of the Spirit is God's new way of working, his new way of making us new. The law with its stern demands was the old way. Paul called it the *dispensation of death*. The law itself was not bad, but it brought judgment because men could not keep it. And the judgment for sin was death.

As attractive as the old law was in expressing God's will, the Spirit's way is infinitely better. He gives us power to do God's will. His ways are the ways of life. The wrappings of the law may be tempting to our childish eyes, but the true gift is God's grace lavished upon our lives by the Holy Spirit. We must not exchange the gift for its package.

The Age of Acquittal

Paul made several specific points as he drew his contrast between the old ways of God and the new ways. For instance,

he contrasted the condemnation of the old with the righteousness of the new: "For if there was splendor in the dispensation of condemnation, the dispensation of righteousness must
far exceed it in splendor" (2 Cor. 3:9).

The law had no choice but to condemn. Its standards were
clear. Men, in either weakness or willfulness, broke them.
Judgment was the result. The law increased guilt; it marked
men and women as rebels against the ways of God; it became
a means of condemnation.

In contrast, the Spirit applies Christ's righteousness to our
lives; he leads us to accept God's forgiveness; he offers divine
pardon. His age, his method of operation, is an age of acquittal.

The choice is obvious. The best prison in the world holds
no attraction for the man who is offered full pardon. Don't
let the old way lure you toward condemnation, when Christ
has granted his acquittal. His righteousness has cleared you
with God. Listen to the Spirit's words of forgiveness. Christ
is faithful and righteous to forgive our sins—that is the motto
of the Spirit's new age (1 John 1:9). Live by it, and you
will live abundantly.

The Age of Permanence

What makes the Spirit's work even greater is that it lasts.
Its permanence puts the age of the Spirit far ahead of the
old age—so far ahead that comparison is futile: "Indeed, in
this case, what once had splendor has come to have no
splendor at all, because of the splendor that surpasses it. For
if what faded away came with splendor, what is permanent
must have much more splendor" (2 Cor. 3:10-11).

Go to Mount Sinai today, and you will see an impressive
mountain. But the glory is gone. God's voice is no longer
heard, and Moses is dead.

In contrast look at the Church, the society of the new age,
the community built by the Spirit. Wherever you go you

find God's people, worshiping and serving, praying and working. In them God's glory shines as bright as ever. He has shared with his Church his permanent splendor.

Fleeting moments of *earthly* glory, most of us have tasted. I remember playing baseball one day in the stadium that was the home of the Oakland Oaks. That must have been thirty-five years ago. I stood at shortstop where one of my heroes played. I even talked to some of the baseball players whose names I still remember. I stood at home plate and batted in the same box that the stars of the league used. Even the fact that I struck out does not dim the glory of those moments. But the three innings that I was assigned to play were soon over, and it was back to the asphalt street in front of our home, back to the gravel playing field at Parker School.

What God offers through the Holy Spirit is a glory that does not fade. The dispensation—the age—of the Spirit is an age of pardon; and that pardon is permanent.

The Age of Freedom

Paul had yet more to say about the new age that God's Spirit brings. Freedom—freedom to enjoy fellowship with God—is one of the great gifts of this age. Here, again, a contrast is drawn between the old age and the new. Moses put a veil over his face because God's glory had shown so brightly on him that his face became a flashing mirror reflecting the glory of God (2 Cor. 3:7). The veil also kept the Israelites from watching the luster of Moses' face grow dim as his mountaintop experience wore off. That veil became, for Paul, a symbol of the inability of the Jews to understand what God was really doing. "Yes, to this day whenever Moses is read a veil lies over their minds; but when a man turns to the Lord the veil is removed. Now the Lord is the Spirit, and where the Spirit of the Lord is, there is freedom" (2 Cor. 3:15–17).

The glory of God was too bright for human beings to take,

even in reflected form from the face of Moses. Understanding who God is and what he is doing is difficult, unless the Spirit of the Lord sets minds free.

When he does, we have liberty to enjoy God's fellowship and to understand his purposes. We have ready access to God through the Spirit who lives within us. My father was a pastor. On the door of his study was a sign "Pastor's Office." Some of the people in our church were timid about opening the door and walking in. I was not. The pastor was my father. I was his son. I enjoyed ready access to him anytime I needed it. I had the freedom to go to him and make my wants known. Openly I went to him to enjoy his fellowship and to understand his will. The Spirit of God gives the sons of God that kind of freedom. It is one of the marks of the new age.

The Age of Renewal

One final word about the new age, the age of the Spirit. Perhaps this is Paul's best word. The Holy Spirit is changing us to be more like Christ! Again Paul drew on the story of Moses, who put the veil over his face because of God's bright glory. He contrasted believers with the Israelites whose minds were veiled just as Moses' face had been: "And we all, with unveiled face, beholding the glory of the Lord, are being changed into his likeness from one degree of glory to another; for this comes from the Lord who is the Spirit" (2 Cor. 3:18).

God's Spirit is on the move. This is his age, the dispensation given over to his work of renewal. The ravages of our sin he is dealing with; our stubborn rebellion he is putting aside; our idols he is breaking up; our arrogant pride he is breaking down; our selfish wills he is making over.

What we were meant to be he is forming. What Christ wants us to be he is working out. Step by step, stage by stage, year by year, he does his work. And what a work it is. "Changed into his likeness"—this is man's highest goal. Beside it everything else pales. In comparison, great fortunes are like heaps of dust; high honors are like worthless trinkets.

Nobel prizes, Academy awards, Congressional medals—these are dime store baubles. To be like Christ—in righteousness and holiness—that is the glory of the new age. The Holy Spirit is making it possible.

How is he doing in your life? Don't miss the gift by letting it get buried in the wrappings. Religious duties, rigid ceremonies, legalistic works belong to the old age, not the new. Let the Spirit who is Lord of the new age catch you up in his new work. Trust Jesus Christ, and watch his Spirit begin to change your life. You will never be the same again.

Prayer: Father, make us sons and daughters of the new age. We have had our fill of the old ways. They failed to satisfy. Your new work is what we want: your pardon, your constant presence, your freedom, your renewing power. Through Christ we dare to ask. Amen.

Conclusion

God at work in the world today—this is the heart of what the Bible teaches about the Holy Spirit. The Sovereign Father has not left the completion of his plan to chance. He, with the Son, has sent the Holy Spirit as the guarantee that the entire divine purpose will be carried out.

To do this God uses the Church—you, me, and millions like us, ordinary human beings with a full measure of human foolishness and frailty. But he does not leave the results to us. He does not risk the success of his program on our power or our obedience. He comes himself in the person of his Spirit and lives with us, equipping, encouraging, convicting.

God not only conducts the orchestra of salvation; he himself plays all the parts. The tone, the tempo, the interpretation are what he wants. God not only coaches the team; he himself plays all the positions. The patterns, the timing, the score are what he desires.

Yet he does all this without making us robots. That is what makes the Church so wonderful. It is God's people, with all our human limitations, filled with God himself through the Holy Spirit to live and serve effectively.

Our task is to apply God's truths to our lives, to believe his promises, to obey his orders, to experience his forgiveness and power, to rejoice in his magnificent gifts to us—and to take no credit for any of this. Salvation from beginning to end, from creation to eternity, is his doing—yet his doing includes our participation. We take no glory. Our glory is to give the glory to him.

Life like this is true human life. Life in God's Spirit is the life for which we were designed, the atmosphere for which we were created. This life—life in the Spirit—speaks to our deepest human longings.

I thought of this when I read *Jonathan Livingston Seagull*, the beautiful parable of a remarkable bird, a bird that longs to move beyond the limitations of the average gull and does. As I read, I pondered the popularity of the little book. What made the airline pilot walking through the cabin say to me, "That's some kind of book"? (Only his language was more graphic than that!). Why have so many millions of people found it attractive?

It is probably only a slight oversimplification to say that Jonathan Gull symbolized their desire to be more than they are by being what they really are. They yearn to tap some inner power, to gain some clearer insight, to spark some nobler motive that will lift them beyond their limitations and make them truly free. They identify with a bird who learned to fly higher and faster and slower than his fellows and who gave himself in loving dedication to teach others to do the same.

The aspirations are noble; nobody should be faulted who shares them. What is wrong is that the search for power is misdirected. Jonathan Livingston Seagull finds his power within his own mind and spirit. He learns to control his body by the concentration of his mind. His spirit breaks through his material restrictions, allowing him to accomplish feats other gulls have not even dreamed of.

From the Bible we learn lessons about our creatureliness and our sinfulness that keep us from holding out false hopes about our own power. We do not look to "the real Jonathan Seagull, who lives within us all" as Richard Bach put it in the dedication of the book. We look to the Holy Spirit of God who can make all things new—even us.

The Bible's point is clear: not the earthly seagull but the heavenly Dove. Through him human wholeness and freedom are possible.